...tispiece for William Booth's book offers a graphic explanation of how the Darkest England scheme is intended to work. The 'submerged tenth' are first rescued by willing Salvationists from their squalor and degradation. They are offered work and shelter in the City Colony before being transferred to the Farm Colony and eventually to the Overseas Colony.

Hadleigh Salvation Army Farm
A Vision Re-born

Also by Gordon Parkhill and Graham Cook

SPIRIT OF THE SEA The Salvation Army in Leigh-on-Sea 1902–2002

Hadleigh
Salvation Army Farm
A Vision Reborn

GORDON PARKHILL AND GRAHAM COOK

SHIELD
BOOKS

Published in 2008 by The Salvation Army

Copyright © 2008 The Salvation Army

ISBN 978-0-85412-776-4

Designed and typeset by Michael T. Harrington
of MATS Typesetters, Southend-on-Sea, Essex
www.typesetter.biz
Book Production by Graham Cook

Printed in Great Britain

Dedication

To:
All those who have lived and worked on
the Farm Colony and in more recent years the
Farm and Training Centre,
and to Laurie Gage whose original
comments inspired this book

Contents

Acknowledgements

The authors would like to acknowledge the help of the following:

Derek Barber, Roger Cowley, Major David Dalziel (IHQ,) Ian Hughes, Michael Harrington, Lieut-Colonel Moira Wright (NZ), George Hazell (Australia), Karl R. Larson (Canada), Lindsay Cox (Australia), Ian Collier (Australia), Gordon Taylor and staff at the International Heritage Centre, London, staff at the local Studies Centre, Southend Library, staff at the Essex Record Office, Chelmsford, Don Watson, Colonel Brindley Boon, Lieut-Colonel Ray Steadman-Allen, Doris Petchey, Paula Thompson, Keith Cakebread, Shelley Carter, Simon Gibson, David Greenwood, Peter and Mildred Howard, Commissioner William Rivers, Robin Bryant, Ingrid Ashcroft, Brian Creasey of Easton Lodge, P.H.C. Day, Betty and Ruby Nickless, The Reverend Doctor Ian Bradley, Greta Groves, Adrian Gascoyne (Essex County Council Countryside Archaeological Adviser), Dr. Jock Cook, the late Laurie Gage, Mrs Colonel Joyce Swansbury, Peter Wexham, Alf Lowrey, Shirley Coulson-Broom and Brian Snow.

Authors' Note

The last known guide to the Farm Colony was produced in the 1920s. Since then unfortunately many Salvation Army records have been either lost or destroyed.

Piecing together the story of William Booth's ambitious social project has therefore not been easy, and at times frustrating. However we have found it a story well worth telling, trying to recreate the work and lives of so many people. In a task of this kind omissions are inevitable, some mistakes also. Perhaps some who read this may be able to fill in the gaps and correct the errors. For our part, we will be only too pleased if they are able to do so.

Introduction

THE STORY OF THE Hadleigh Farm Colony, or to give it its original name, The Hadleigh Land and Industrial Colony, begins in 1890 with the publication of William Booth's book *In Darkest England and the Way Out*. Buying farmland in this part of Essex was to be the fulfilment of the second part of Booth's scheme to deal with the appalling social problems caused by extreme poverty and long-term unemployment. Hadleigh was to be the Farm Colony, with the City Colony and the Overseas Colony forming the other two parts of the scheme. It was the place chosen for a daring, not to say risky, social experiment.

Today, on the same land and with the same sense of vision, The Salvation Army is seeking to meet the needs of the early twenty-first century. A training centre, started in 1990, aims to provide practical help for those with special training needs. A tea room, open to the public, as well as offering one of the best views in South East Essex, gives people an opportunity to see at first hand how those needs are being met. A monthly farmers' market that provides local farmers and producers with an attractive venue has proved equally popular. The farm itself, under its enterprising manager, is run in an environmentally friendly way, and is looking to promote organically grown crops wherever possible. The Rare Breeds Centre attracts and delights children and adults alike. Hadleigh Farm today is truly a vision reborn.

1. Colony entrance (*opposite*) before the First World War.

2. The People's Mission Hall was previously a market in Whitechapel. William Booth converted it into his main meeting hall and centre for the distribution of cheap food for the poor. It became the headquarters of the East London Christian Mission and then The Salvation Army until 1881, when it moved to 101 Queen Victoria Street.

CHAPTER ONE

What was a Farm Colony and why Hadleigh?

WILLIAM BOOTH was in many respects a late convert to the social work of The Salvation Army. The first headquarters of the East London Christian Mission in the Whitechapel Road had included a soup kitchen. In January 1867 Booth had written 'We are now giving away soup and bread, and propose doing so while distress continues and funds are sent us.' However by the mid 1870s The Christian Mission had given up soup kitchens and food shops, and certainly by the early 1880s when the Christian Mission had become The Salvation Army, Booth was having second thoughts about gratuitous hand-outs.

Then came his 'London Bridge experience,' when it is said that on his return late on a Sunday night from a weekend evangelistic campaign he noticed from his cab window men sleeping out on the bridge and along the Embankment. The following day he asked his son Bramwell if he knew about this problem, and when Bramwell said he did he asked what his son was going to do about it. This was late in the year 1887 and the following year the Army's first Men's Food and Shelter Depot was opened in the West India Dock Road, a place which was to provide important relief during the London Dock strike of 1889. This time however, the meals had to be paid for, although at a greatly subsidised price. More food and shelter depots were opened in 1889 and by 1893 nearly 4,000,000 meals were being provided each year.

Alongside the food and shelter depots came the elevators or Salvation Army workshops. Their aim was to make it unnecessary for the homeless or unemployed to be compelled to go into the workhouse; that wretched place of last resort for so many of the 'submerged tenth' of the population. Workshops allowed a man to earn sufficient to pay for his food and lodging in an Army Shelter. Then, as he demonstrated his worth, he was 'elevated' to a better class of accommodation; a scheme which was to be repeated when the Land and Industrial Colony at Hadleigh was set up. No more gratuitous hand-outs, this was the Victorian doctrine of self-help in action. The Army also opened its own

3. William Booth, Founder. b.1829 d.1912

4. W. Bramwell Booth, General 1912–1929

5. Castle Farm.
This line drawing
and the one
below appeared
in The Salvation
Army journal
All The World
in 1893.

labour bureau at this time, offering employers and the unemployed a place to meet. This anticipated by some twenty years the Government's own scheme of labour exchanges. food and shelter depots, elevators and labour bureaux were all essential elements of Booth's Darkest England Scheme.

The Darkest England Scheme had three parts to it. It began with The City Colony where The Salvation Army would use its many social institutions to rescue those drowning in a sea of poverty and degradation, as the illustrated frontispiece of the Booth's book so graphically demonstrates. Those deemed suitable would then be transferred to the Farm Colony where they would be offered training in various forms of work, principally agriculture and brick making. This was intended to be an industrial as well as a farm colony. Finally those who couldn't be found employment at home would have the Army's help to find work in the Overseas Colony, the final part of the scheme.

Although 'Darkest England' does not refer specifically to Hadleigh it does mention Essex. Booth speaks of the possibilities and advantages for his scheme of 'our Essex cornlands.' The Army's evangelistic work was already established at this time in Shoeburyness and neighbouring Southend. The area was not unfamiliar in Army circles.

By the late 19th century many farmers were suffering the effects of a severe agricultural depression. They were only too willing to sell their land to any reasonable bidder. The farmland around Hadleigh was notorious for its poor quality; known locally as the Hadleigh badlands. In 'Darkest England' William Booth stated 'My present idea is to take an estate from 500 to a 1,000 acres within reasonable distance of London. It should be of such land as will be suitable for market gardening, while having some clay on it for brick making and for crops requiring a heavier soil. If possible, it should not only be on a line of railway which is managed by intelligent and progressive directors, but it should have access to the sea and the river.' He could hardly have found a more suitable site than Hadleigh. The only drawback, apart from the poor quality of the land and its slope towards the river, was his stipulation that the Colony should be 'planted clear out in the open away from the public house, that upas tree of civilisation'.

6. Cow Sheds.

The village of Hadleigh, not far from the farmland, already had its pubs. A upas tree, incidentally, was a Javanese tree of a particularly poisonous variety.

Despite these potential disadvantages, the availability of three adjacent farms, Castle Farm, Park Farm and Sayers Farm, situated between the road to London and the River Thames offered William Booth the 900 acres he was seeking. The scene was set for his radical social experiment.

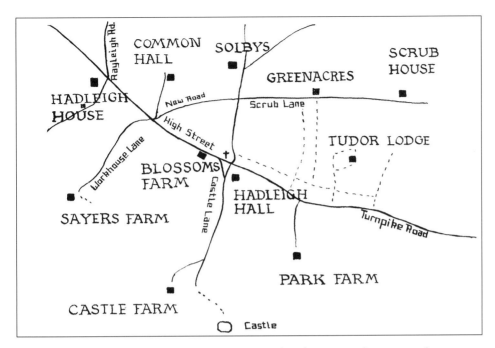

7. The location of Sayer's Farm, Castle Farm and Park Farm can be seen on this map, as well as other properties in Hadleigh, also bought by The Salvation Army.

8. Castle House (built 1706). Once Castle Farm and renamed Home Farm. This house had accommodation for up to 30 men, they would progress from the dormitories and work their way up to Castle House, where they would find tidy rooms and privacy as a reward. This property was pulled down in 1974.

9. Park House. Listed originally as a boarding establishment in the centre of the fruit and vegetable garden. Officers occasionally stayed there, but it was open to all visitors. This residence has a fine view over the estuary, the colony and castle, but this photo taken in 2007 shows the house empty and boarded up. It was at one time the residence of the Governor of the Colony. The Salvation Army has plans for this property.

10. Sayer's Farm. Named after one-time owner William Sayer. This was the residence of the Farm Superintendent, buildings around the farm included stables and piggeries. Also kept here were the best horses, the famous Colony Shire mares and was the location of the Colony dairy.

11. This map dated 1896 shows how the Hadleigh Colony spread down the London Road into neighbouring Leigh-on-Sea to take in Leigh Park Farm and Leigh Heath Farm either side of the London Road. North of the London road became the Highlands estate, and to the south, the Leigh Heath estate now known as the Marine Estate. Leigh Marsh Farm was another farm bought by the Army.

12. Four early governors of the colony. Commissioner Elijah Cadman, Colonel William Stitt, Colonel Wright and Colonel David Lamb, with the first head office in the centre of the picture.

CHAPTER TWO

The Colony at Work 1891-1914

'I CAN WELL IMAGINE the incredulous laughter which will greet my proposal. "What," it will be said, "Do you think you can create agricultural pioneers out of the scum of Cockneydom?"'

This was exactly what William Booth was proposing and furthermore, he was convinced it would work. There were indeed those who not only greeted the scheme with incredulous laughter, but others who were much more vitriolic in their opposition. In the early years of its growth The Salvation Army was not universally popular. One of its leading opponents at this time was Professor Thomas Huxley, who detested everything about the Army and was deeply suspicious of Booth's motives in setting up his Darkest England Scheme. Equally suspicious, and at first, equally hostile, were the villagers of Hadleigh; a small community clustered round its Norman church. The arrival of The Salvation Army, accompanied by its contingent of 'down and outs', the flotsam and jetsam of East London, was most certainly not welcome. The strength of opposition may be gleaned from reports in the local newspaper. In the course of time most of the local opposition subsided as the worst fears of the villagers failed to materialise and a number even found work on the Army Colony.

The £100,000 Booth believed he needed to buy the land and set up the scheme was raised within three months. Booth certainly had his supporters as well as his opponents. A conversation between Commissioner Cadman, who became the Governor of the Colony, and the editor of the local newspaper, the *Southend Standard* in April 1891 underlines the importance of the proximity of the River Thames for water transport. The landing stages and wharves mentioned in that article were quickly built, and the remains of the wooden piers can still be seen by anyone walking the sea-wall footpath between Leigh-on-Sea and Benfleet. The running expenses of the Colony were considerably reduced by an ingenious use of raw materials obtained from salvage brought by Thames sailing barge from the Army's own wharf at Battersea, part of the City Colony.

13. Hadleigh High Street, how it looked about the time The Salvation Army arrived.

14. Commissioner Elijah Cadman, Colony Governor.

15. Locomotive and barges belonging to the Colony. This illustration is of a Peckett engine, which was delivered to the colony in 1894 and was built in Bristol. The engine's livery was green and was driven by a Mr Williams.

By March 1891 the three farms making up the original 900 acres had been purchased at a cost of £12,000.

Construction work on the Colony was begun by Staff Captain Alderton with 48 pioneers from the East End of London. Wooden dormitories were soon built, an agricultural steam engine was bought, and potatoes, mangelwurzels, swedes and garden produce were sown. By June 1891, 45 Colonists had arrived, and by December there were nearly 250. By that time also a dining room had been added together with a wash-house, laundry, houses for officers, a 16-bed hospital and a Citadel for worship. Rapid progress indeed!

One of the most astonishing achievements was the development of the transport system. Tramlines nearly four miles long, connected the three farms to the wharf on Hadleigh Ray. The tramway, however, was narrow gauge and not suitable for moving bricks from the three brick works which were in operation by the autumn of 1892. Therefore a standard gauge railway was built from the bottom of Elevator Hill connecting with brickfields one and two. The line was then carried by an embankment and bridge over the London, Tilbury and Southend railway line to the wharf. Brickfield three which was at the top of Elevator Hill near Sayers Farm, was connected to the standard gauge line by a narrow gauge double tramway which tackled the hill by the loaded wagons pulling up the empty ones, a somewhat precarious but effective arrangement. Sadly, little remains today of this amazing enterprise, apart from the brick piers of the bridge which carried the Army's engines, 'Prosperity' and 'Queen Mary' down to the wharf.

It soon became apparent that the original 900 acres were insufficient for the Colony's aims and other farms were purchased during the 1890s. These included Leigh Park Farm, Leigh Heath Farm and Leigh Marsh Farm. These purchases extended the Colony land from Hadleigh into neighbouring Leigh-on-Sea. They also increased the land owned by William Booth to over 3,000 acres. This extended ownership had some unusual and unexpected results. The Army found itself the owner of the land on which the Leigh cockle sheds stood. Thus it was to the Army that the cocklers had to turn when their livelihood was threatened by the development plans of the Leigh Gas Works. Ironically, two of the dispossessed cocklers were Salvationists; the Livermore brothers of the Leigh-on-Sea Corps. Another consequence is that, even today, prospective buyers of property on the Highlands and Marine estates in Leigh-on-Sea discover that the presence of William Booth's name on their title deeds brings with it certain prohibitions, including the sale of alcohol.

The booklet about the Colony called *Hadleigh: The Story of a Great Endeavour* produced in 1902, explained the object of the Colony as being 'To give employment (and food and lodging in return for his labour) to any able-bodied man who is willing to work. This irrespective of nationality and creed.' However it was the definition of able-bodied which was often the problem. Colonel Lamb, who wrote the 1902 book whilst Governor of the Colony, defined this as

16. Commissioner David C. Lamb, became Governor from 1898 at the age of 32. He is photographed here in his Aberdeen University Robe and Doctor of Law sash. He was a pioneer of social change.

17. Leigh Park Farm. When a man came to the colony, usually in a bad condition through alcohol and unhealthy eating and through sleeping rough, he would be set light work at Leigh Park which was about a mile from the farm offices. After a month or two he would then be brought to the main Colony to work. There was accommodation here for 40 men.

18. The farm house as it is today; two cottages, situated on the corner of Walker Drive and Olive Avenue, part of the Highlands Estate. Leigh Park was a hundred acres divided into a market garden, fruit orchard and pasture land.

19. General William Booth inspecting the colony on horseback c.1896.

20. Blacksmith's Forge.

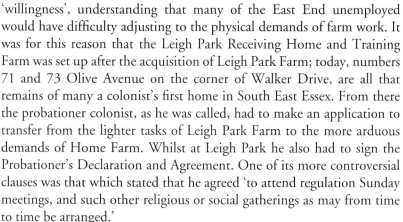

'willingness', understanding that many of the East End unemployed would have difficulty adjusting to the physical demands of farm work. It was for this reason that the Leigh Park Receiving Home and Training Farm was set up after the acquisition of Leigh Park Farm; today, numbers 71 and 73 Olive Avenue on the corner of Walker Drive, are all that remains of many a colonist's first home in South East Essex. From there the probationer colonist, as he was called, had to make an application to transfer from the lighter tasks of Leigh Park Farm to the more arduous demands of Home Farm. Whilst at Leigh Park he also had to sign the Probationer's Declaration and Agreement. One of its more controversial clauses was that which stated that he agreed 'to attend regulation Sunday meetings, and such other religious or social gatherings as may from time to time be arranged.'

This element of compulsion, whilst not to the liking of everyone, including some of the Colony's many visitors, did not prevent those like author Rider Haggard and socialist Beatrice Webb from expressing their admiration for what was being achieved. The latter, who visited Hadleigh in 1908 said when speaking of the Colony's officers, 'A beautiful spirit of love and personal service, of content and joy permeates the service; there is a persistent note of courtesy to others.' Three years earlier, Rider Haggard, himself a Norfolk landowner as well as a writer, admired the energy of the work force and what had been achieved with land of such poor quality. Among the various departments he might well have visited would have included the farm itself, both arable and pasture, the market garden, the poultry section, the pottery and the brickfields as well as the maintenance department with its different workshops including a blacksmith's forge. In all there were nine departments each managed by a Superintendent who in turn was responsible to the Governor.

A less well-known part of the Colony's work at this time was that it contracted out its work-force to other parts of Essex. Mr Wilkins of Tiptree employed

22. THE COUNTESS OF WARWICK spoke at The Salvation Army, Regent Hall, London in 1908, giving her views on the unemployed and the social work of The Salvation Army. With her were Commissioner David Lamb and Land colonists. She said '... a bond of friendship has been formed between myself and Hadleigh by a band of seventy Hadleigh Colonists who are at present laying out a garden near my house at Easton Lodge. I should like to take this opportunity of stating publicly that the work and conduct of the men have justified the experiment far beyond my highest expectations...'

21. Carpenter's Shop.

colonists to pick strawberries for his famous Tiptree jam and was so impressed by the quality of their work that he persuaded his fellow Congregationalists to let the Army have a piece of land in the village on which to build a citadel. Even more impressive were the colonists' achievements in the gardens of Easton Lodge. Here they were used by Harold Peto, a famous landscape gardener, who had been commissioned by the Countess of Warwick to lay out the grounds of her Essex home. As the distance between the gardens near Dunmow and Hadleigh was too great for daily travel, dormitories were built to accommodate the workers. So impressed was the Countess by their hard work that she invited the men to put on their Sunday best and join her in her home for her daughter's 'coming out' party. The occasion was described in the *Daily News* of January 1903.

'The Countess of Warwick recently entertained the whole body of Salvation Army workmen to the number of seventy, now employed in extending the landscape gardens at Easton Lodge, her ladyship's Essex seat. The workmen, who number amongst them broken professional men, decayed tradesmen and others of 'the submerged tenth,' have been engaged on the estate at Easton for the past month, and appear to be very contented in the employ of the Countess. A sumptuous dinner was laid for the men in the grand ballroom erected for the society function connected with the 'coming out' of the Hon. Lady Marjorie Greville, the only daughter of the Earl and Countess. Dressed in the best their scanty wardrobe could offer, the men, whose ages ranged from 19 to 50 – a motley group of professedly converted – were ushered into the presence of the Countess and her house guests, from whom they received a kindly welcome. A varied entertainment followed the dinner.' The present owner of Easton Lodge, Mr Brian Creasey, is in the process of restoring the gardens after many years of neglect. A notice in the grounds and a folder in his small museum refer to the work carried out by the Colonists so many years ago.

In 1912, 21 years after the start of the Colony, a set of statistics was published showing that altogether nearly 7,000 men had been admitted to Hadleigh, of whom nearly 200 had remained on the farm as employees. Over 4,000 had gone on to other employment and 400 had emigrated. The one great disappointment of the Darkest England Scheme was that the overseas Colony failed to materialise. There was too much local opposition in the British colonies to Booth's dream of settling his 'down-and-outs' in their territories. However The Salvation Army's own emigration schemes were already established well before the colony itself was set up. The first group to emigrate from Hadleigh left in 1901. By 1905 the Army was chartering its own steamships and amongst their passengers would be those from Hadleigh.

By the outbreak of the First World War the Colony had already

THE GLADE
(FORMERLY THE JAPANESE GARDEN)

This area was laid out in the winter of 1902/3 as a Japanese garden. The construction labour force were from the Salvation Army Inebriates Home at Hadleigh near Southend. These 67 men carried out all this work during an Essex winter on heavy clay soil; tens of thousands of tons of soil were shifted.
The highs and lows of this area were sculpted out by these men, right down to the lakes at the far end of the glade. Some of Harold Peto's original planting can still be seen, the Corsican pines, limes and other species on the perimeter. Trees of about 50 years of age were planted by Maynard Greville in the 1950s. Further planting was done by us in 1997/98.
Originally large rocks were placed throughout the garden with occasional Japanese features such as lanterns; these have long been removed. There was a thatched Japanese tea-house on the top lake.
Today, we have cleared hundreds, if not thousands of trees which had sprung up since W.W.II and have now laid the area to grass. Tree planting is going on apace, to be followed by shrubs. Many bulbs are also being planted. Unfortunately, the lakes are not part of the garden, as the Dunmow Fishing Club have been here for 40 years and have a continuing lease.
However we are creating a 'CLAIREVOIE' or 'TENBONDAI' (viewing platform) to give a focal point to this far end of the gardens. It may be that in the course of time a Japanese garden is created in this area.
To walk down this lush, green glade will be to experience a sense of calm and serenity – and a romantic feel for the past.

23. The Glade, formerly the Japanese Garden at Easton Lodge, was laid out in the winter of 1902/3 by Salvation Army Colony workers as indicated on this plaque in the garden.

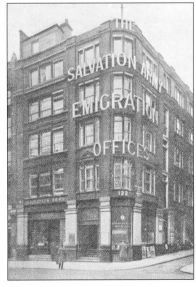

24. Emigration Offices, at 122 Queen Victoria Street, London.

experienced a number of changes. The internal railway had closed for reasons that are not entirely clear and at least one of the brickfields was no longer in use. Although the Royal Commission on the Poor Laws, which sat in 1908, fell short of recommending state aid for Booth's scheme, it was full of high praise for its achievements. At the same time the Liberal government, which had set up the Commission, was pushing ahead with its own programme of social change. Non-contributory old-age pensions were introduced in 1909 along with labour exchanges. The Salvation Army, incidentally, had already set up its own labour exchanges as previously mentioned. Two years later the government introduced sickness insurance for those in work and a limited scheme of unemployment insurance. As the old Poor Law system began to change, and the first signs of a welfare state began to emerge, the reasons for continuing with social projects like Hadleigh became less urgent.

25. 'Bon Voyage'. The first group to emigrate from Hadleigh was in 1901. By 1905 the Army was chartering its own steamships. This photo shows a party of women and boys leaving Tilbury to join an Australian bound ship.

26. The Lamb family grave can be found in Leigh cemetery. It highlights the active roles that both the Commissioner and Mrs Lamb played in the life of Southend even after he ceased being Governor of the Colony. He is buried here with his wife Minnie Clinton Lamb, JP and two of their children. David, their eldest son, died of heart failure at the age of 19 in 1909, and Patrick, their youngest son, was killed in action during the First World War in 1918.

27. Stitt. The family grave of William Samuel Stitt (1857–1930) early governor of the colony and his wife Mary Jane (d.1926) can be found in the graveyard of Hadleigh church, along with the graves of other colony staff, employees and colonists.

THE COLONIST

Published for our own pleasure and instruction

Nº 6   February 15 1892.   Gratis

As Others See Us.

The "Weekly Bulletin."

a journal of Finance, Mining and Instruction says:—

"Still in Essex as I write these lines. To-day I have walked mile after mile through a district yet unknown to me & always the same sad, sad tale. Field after field un-tilled, house after house fallen or falling to pieces. Farms that afforded existence & happiness to generation after generation, all tumbling to pieces, and as to cottages, many of the roofs (even when they are inhabited) are open to the daylight. Ah God! can such things be?

But stay— what is this! Impossible! My vision must be mad— dancing mad! What do I see or think I see? I scarce dare look; but yet surely I do see men & carts and horses, and new gates and clipped hedges! And hear whistling, whistling, ye gods, and songs— why, I never such in Essex before! But my eye travels on and on, and true or not seems to embrace within its vision hundreds nearly of acres of cabbages, or wurzels, or turnips, or vegetation of one sort or another with dozens or scores of ablebodied men, laborers or non-laborers but all at work somehow! And now that I am nearer I see buildings of every description erected, or in course of erection I see the fields are ploughed-yes, actually ploughed, and I dance as I hear the dear old whistle of an agricultural steam engine. But what does it mean? At the moment I ask myself this question, I see close & a notice board that

28. An early edition of the Colony's own newspaper.

29. An Article in the August 1891 edition of *The Deliverer*, a publication which recorded Salvation Army Rescue Work, provides an illuminating snapshot of the colony within a few months of its foundation. It records the visit of the editor of the paper together with a Major Stitt, described as 'a sort of Godfather to the Colony', later to become its Governor, travelling with four travelling bags, a cornet case, one or two parcels, a bundle of books, three or four milk pans and a couple of fenders, clearly vital supplies in the Colony's early days. A huge hoarding of red, white and blue erected in a field to the left first announced to them that they were on Salvation Army ground, and a little further on a farm wagon left them in no doubt as to their whereabouts, painted large on the side panel 'William Booth Hadleigh'.

Their welcome meal included honey as well as fruit and vegetables, all home grown. This was the first piece of honeycomb from the newly established hives. This was just one indication of how quickly the Colony was up and running. Other evidence of this gleaned by the visitors included the 200 goslings, 57 head of cattle, 130 sheep, 13 horses and 5 foals and 70 pigs. At this time the Colony was under the direction of Mr Harold Moore, its Consulting Director. He had set out its objectives which included: 1. The carrying on of an ordinary farm growing more especially the produce required for consumption by the labourers. 2. Training incompetent and destitute men so they may become capable emigrants, or outdoor English labourers. 3. Finding profitable work on the land for as many as possible who required work. 4. Carrying on industrial work under more healthy conditions than in the London workshops.

The visitors asked Mr Moore what sort of men came to the colony. 'All sorts come, those who have been accustomed to farm labour and those who haven't, mostly the latter, but they are all voluntary'. He explained the system of grants which took the place of actual wages. The number of colonists at the time of the visit was 65 but by the time the article was published the number had increased to 155. As this early stage of the Colony's history the colonists took their meals in a tent, in which worship also took place. A barn was being used as a temporary dormitory while the more permanent buildings were being erected. The Colony's Sunday services were by all accounts attracting 'country folk from all the villages around'. The visitors also discovered that whereas attendance at the services had originally been optional, it was now 'deemed advisable to call the roll', a point which as mentioned earlier in the chapter led to a certain amount of controversy and adverse comment.

The article finished by the editors making an appeal for items which would make the colonists' lives more comfortable and less spartan.

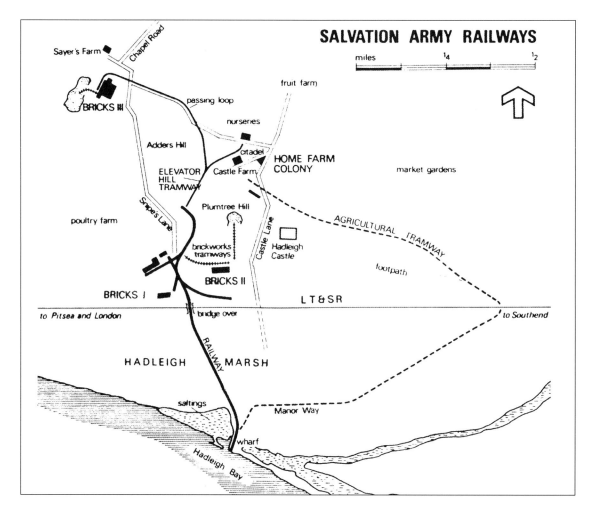

SALVATION ARMY RAILWAYS

30. Salvation Army Railways. A narrow gauge tramway was built in 1891, three and a three quarter miles in length joining Leigh station with the three farms. It was suitable for carrying agricultural produce and was in the shape of a giant hairpin from the colony to the wharf. On 8 June 1892 the LTSR (London, Tilbury and Southend Railway) came to an arrangement with General William Booth to construct a bridge across the railway line at Hadleigh. If a standard gauge railway line was to be built, something more substantial was required than a tramline. By the end of that year a locomotive was reported at work and bricks were being produced with access to the barges at Hadleigh Ray. The brickworks were organised in three centres; BRICKS I. lay just north of the bridge and consisted of clay pits and several kilns. A red, wire-cut brick, suitable for bridge, sewer and engineering work was made at this yard with an output of 150,000 bricks per week.

BRICKS II to the east, produced a Yellow London stocks-brick and the output could be as much as 4m bricks per year, but this was restricted to half that due to water supply restrictions. It was situated on Plumtree Hill, with a short double tramway down to some more pits, kilns and pottery. BRICKS III was north of Bricks I on the west side, below Sayer's Farm. It was connected to the railway by a narrow gauge tramway which followed a circular route via the outskirts of Home Farm then descending down the hill by a double track incline down Elevator Hill. This yard turned out a red brick suitable for villa building with an output of 60,000 per week. Bricks were originally fired in the open, but kilns were soon built.

The earlier tramway was lifted by 1895 by which time a line to Bricks III had been laid. The main line which had been built on a embankment made from London rubbish, brought down by barge from Battersea, crossed the LTSR line by the bridge, across Hadleigh Marsh and reached the wharf on the creek of Hadleigh Ray where barges loaded and unloaded bricks, coal and London refuse. This is a summary of an article which, together with the map, appeared in the Industrial Railways Record, June 1982.

31. Excavating in the brickfields, showing also the colony's extensive tramway system as seen on the map on page 16.

32. Operating brick making machinery.

Scenes at the Wharf in Hadleigh Ray are a reminder that it was an Industrial Colony as well as a Farm Colony.

33. Steam engines arriving at the wharf (above and right). The locomotive comes from Bricks I and II and carries bricks across the London, Tilbury and Southend Railway line.

34. Loading bricks for the wharf (left). As early as 1891 up to six barges a week were loaded. The barges returned from London with cargoes of chalk for brick making and house garbage for burning.

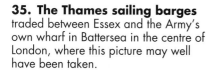

35. The Thames sailing barges traded between Essex and the Army's own wharf in Battersea in the centre of London, where this picture may well have been taken.

36. The brickfields, three operating at one time, were one of the most ambitious parts of William Booth's scheme. Although not without their problems, especially that of water supply, they added a different dimension to the farming operations. Photo (right) Bricks III.

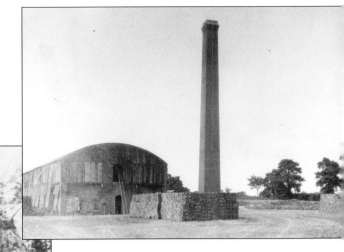

37. Workers digging the clay (left).

38. A scene in the clay pit with workers standing on the tramway (right).

39. Possibly Bricks III, with Well number 1, near Sayer's Farm. With an increase in population and stock at the Colony more water was urgently needed.

40. Salvation Army Land and Industrial Colony S.A.L.I.C. and S.A.F.C. bricks and a milk bottle. WB – William Booth's initials were also featured on the bricks.

41. Brickmaking machinery being operated.

42. The scenes captured (above and below) from an early guide book to the Colony, were clearly intended to demonstrate that a colonist's life was not an easy alternative to unemployment.

43. Commissioner Cadman seen on the site of one of the brickfields, close to the London, Tilbury and Southend Railway. Part of the Colony's own railway system can be clearly seen.

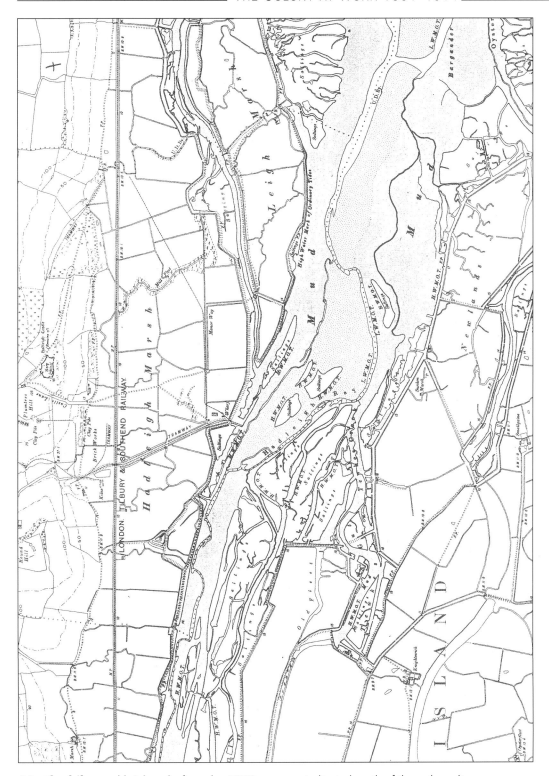

44. The kilns and brickworks from the 1898 map are indicated north of the railway line.

45. Commissioner Cadman, responsible for the Army's social work as well as, at one time, Governor of the Colony, seen here in the centre of the group.

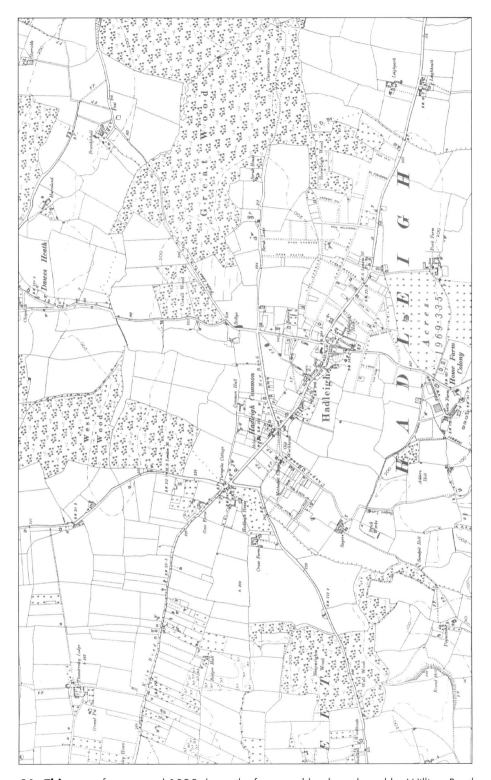

46. This map from around 1895 shows the farms and land purchased by William Booth.

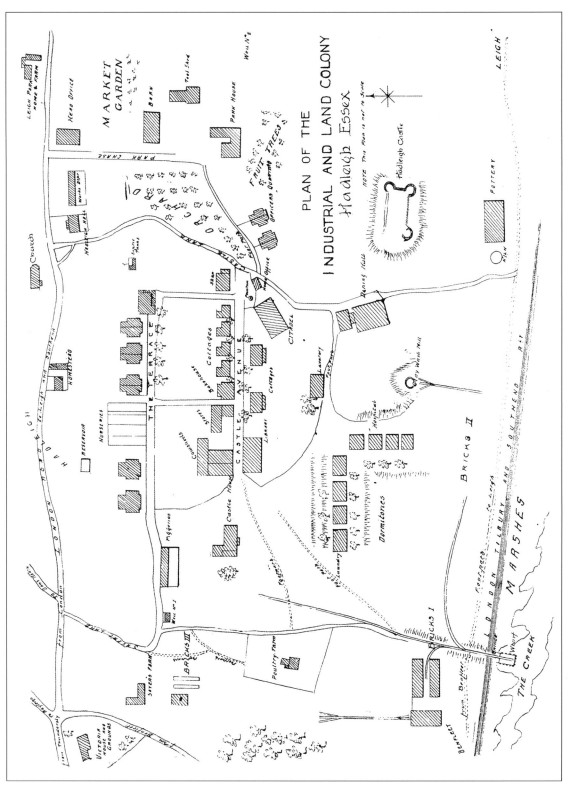

47. Plan of Colony, from the 1902 Guide. As well as the 3 farms it shows the various properties the Army acquired in Hadleigh itself, Florence

July 30, 1892.   THE WAR CRY.   3

A DAY ON THE FARM.

THE FIELD COMMISSIONER SHEPHERDS A GIGANTIC FLOCK

O'ER COLONY "PASTURES NEW" AND TO THE SOUL'S "STILL WATERS."

"Beautiful weather. Little rain yesterday. Ground dry."

That was the wire which the Field Commissioner made it her business to send off to The General almost before she had marshalled her first train full of light-hearted London soldiers out of Leigh Station and formed them up before the eyes of the astonished townsfolk, last Monday morning.

Sunday's rains, so steady and drenching in London, had fallen lightly, it would seem, over Hadleigh Colony, for the Field Commissioner's motherly fears lest her gigantic flock should find muddy roads, dripping hedges and damp grass, were far from realised. Bright sunshine fell on jubilant faces, where, aided by Majors Higgins and Lawrence, with a host of London and Garrison staff, she formed a ring at the Church Corner and began an open-air which lasted while the second, third and fourth trains were unloading their two thousand five hundred excursionists.

SALVATION IN THE CASTLE COURT.

Fire a volley for the Field Commissioner!

48. A visit to Hadleigh by Commissioner Evangeline Booth when Field Commissioner in 1892. At this time the ownership of Castle Farm included the castle itself.

49. The Entrance (*above*) to the Colony. The Citadel was still in the same place in 2000, but has since been demolished.

50. The Entrance (*right*), taken in the 1970s, is to a working farm rather than a farm colony.

51. The two photographs (*below*) taken between the turn of the century and 1910.

The Citadel where the Colony staff, employees and colonists all worshipped together was demolished in 2003. On its site, an extension to the training centre and a new tea room is being built. The Citadel can still be seen however, in all these photographs.

52. Officers from The Salvation Army Assurance Company marching down Castle Lane. They were amongst the many visitors to the Colony.

53. An early view of Castle Lane showing the road unmade.

54. Head Office. An early photograph *c.* 1900 when It was situated in Park Chase, close to the junction with the London Road.

55. Colonel Charles Barker's funeral cortege, May 1901, outside the head office. Major Barker went to Australia in 1883 to expand the work in the colonies. He commenced the Prison-Gate Brigade operating out of Melbourne Gaol. The P-GB Home in Carlton, opened in 1883, is officially The Salvation Army's first social institution in the world. He was recalled to England in 1892, but died of an illness some nine years later.

56. Even today there is a gate where the children are standing in the road, leading up to the castle. The buildings behind at the rear of the Citadel and the Dining Hall.

58. Hadleigh Hall. This property was situated on the corner of Castle Lane and London Road, the site now occupied by a row of shops. It became the Colony Governor's residence but in 1937 was leased to Dr. William James who opened a surgery in partnership with Dr. Samuel McGladdery, it was demolished in 1961.

57. The Homestead. Formerly known as 'Blossoms', this was one of the properties in Hadleigh Village purchased by The Salvation Army where some unmarried employees lived.

59. A number of colony buildings can be seen in this picture including the Head Office after it moved from Park Chase, the 'new' Dining Hall and the Citadel.

60. A similar view taken recently showing part of the Rare Breeds Farm and the Tea Room, built on to the back of the Boys' Dining Hall.

61. Hadleigh Hay Barns, this photograph taken in 1955

62. Barns old and new reveal also distant views across the Thames to Kent with the North Downs in the far distance and Canvey Island to the right.

63. Stalls for the horses inside one of the older barns.

64. One of the original barns but photographed here in 1955.

These photographs show a mixture of the barns built with the help of various grants as well as some of the older brick built ones.

65. Workers receiving a lesson in sowing from George Watson (centre, behind the horse).

66. Ploughing with the Colony's shire horses; there were five in total. This ploughing team is at work on the field which runs along side the London Road.

67. Spraying the fruit trees and **68.** working the field. The orchards formed an important part of the Market Garden whose Superintendent for many years was George Watson.

69. Learning the intricacies of the farm's many machines was one of the more demanding jobs on the farm. George Watson (centre) with two farm hands.

71. Brick worker J. Richards taking a break.

70. The Bell, which once hung above the office entrance called everyone to work in the morning.

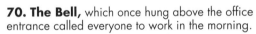

72. A group of farm hands *c.* 1900.

73. Colony coinage. Food could be purchased by means of tokens, like the one illustrated here. They ranged in value from half-pennies to fourpence pieces.

74. The Citadel. One of the earliest photos *c.* 1895 and referred to as 'an important part of The Army's machine for making men'.

75. Magnificent tomatoes hanging in clusters. These glasshouses had heating pipes.

76. The glasshouses were an important part of the market garden.

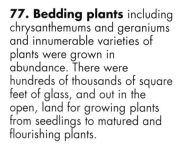

77. Bedding plants including chrysanthemums and geraniums and innumerable varieties of plants were grown in abundance. There were hundreds of thousands of square feet of glass, and out in the open, land for growing plants from seedlings to matured and flourishing plants.

78. Attending to the pigs. Hadleigh's pedigree pigs gained a nationwide reputation for their quality.

79. The piggeries were situated along Seaview Terrace on the left hand side. This view shows the south side of the buildings. There were also piggeries by the Market Garden.

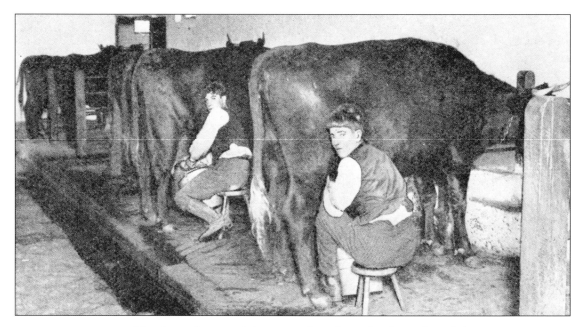

80. The Dairy Herd, known as the Reliance herd, was based close to Sayer's Farm house at the bottom of Chapel Lane. Parts of the buildings remain today.

81. The famous Hadleigh poultry farm where once Cecil Rhodes purchased birds to take back with him to South Africa. These chicken houses gives some indication of the size and variety of the Colony's farming operations.

82. Refreshment building erected in 1895 for the convenience of visitors.

83. The first hospital was in these buildings
which later became employees dwellings.

84. Dormitories varied in comfort, according to the degree of progress which the
colonist made. There were eight in number.

85. The Dormitories, dining room and reading room were erected soon after the purchase of the Colony in 1891, offering fine views of Canvey Island and the Thames.

86. A lending library, near the dormitories, was maintained by the Army for use by the colonists.

87. The first dormitory in which the colonist sleeps.

88. Laundry room *c.*1902 All the washing was done by men, those being chosen were not strong enough to work outside in all weathers.

89. The hospital. An eight bed hospital set up in 1891 had a resident nurse and qualified practitioner. The hospital was under the supervision of a Leigh Doctor who visited twice a week – apparently there had never been an epidemic in the colony.

90. Castle House can be seen at the end of the main street or Castle Avenue, looking from the entrance to the Colony, Photo *c.* 1902.

91. Officers' residences on the right, built with corrugated iron with attractive pickett fencing, affectionately known as 'Tin Street', part of Castle Avenue.

92. The Citadel, where meetings were held, is on the left hand side of Castle Avenue, the main street. Built at a cost of £630, it was one of the largest buildings. There was no aggressive evangelism, but The Salvation Army would not be acting according to its principles if it did not make the religious influence felt.

93. Inside view of the Citadel, which could seat up to 500 people. The two coke burning stoves, the only original form of heating, can be seen on either side of the hall.

94. Another view of the inside of the Citadel. The pictures of William and Catherine Booth, on either side of Christ, were a common feature in Salvation Army halls.

95. The fountain. Erected in 1901 to commemorate the laying on of water to the colony from No.1 well and presented by J. E. Milholland of New York in December that year.

96. The restored fountain in 2000 with the top piece missing.

97. West View. This also included dormitary accommodation and for a time was used as a farmhouse by Peter Howard and his family. Pulled down in 2002.

98. An early photograph taken just inside the gate. The fountain, a gift from the USA and still in the same position, can be seen on the right.

99. The Colony band, ready to march away at the head of a funeral procession in Hadleigh village.

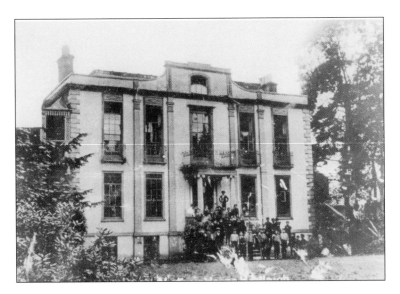

100. Victoria House (previously Hadleigh House but renamed by the Army) was purchased and licensed as a voluntary retreat under the Inebriants Acts of 1879 and 1899. It opened in 1901 and men paid twenty shillings per week, no drugs were administered and inmates were expected to work for up to 30 hours a week on the colony. Only the name survives today as the road junction Victoria House Corner.

101. A Bedroom inside the house.

102. Inmates relaxing in the lounge.

103. The Colony Band with Corps Officers 1902

104. A further picture of the Colony band with Bandmaster Halsey, which became very well known, not only locally but in other parts of The Salvation Army world.

105. Hadleigh Church St James the Less. Colonists served on the Parish Council as the colony became accepted. They were welcome at church services and some were buried in the church graveyard. Some of the first fruit and vegetables and a sheaf of barley was presented at the Harvest Festival, 27 September 1891.

106. Harvest festival procession along Castle Lane, Hadleigh.

107. A corner of Hadleigh churchyard, given over to burials of the colonists as well as officers and employees. This large gravestone erected in 1900 to the memory of colonists is in fact two sided; top left shows an early photo with names clearly visible but the same gravestone, top right, photographed in 2007 shows the ravages of time. On the reverse, dated 1912, some names can still be seen.

108. Colony boys often visited the local people. Here we see Rebecca Snow with two lads outside her house in Short Road, off Castle Lane.

CHAPTER THREE

World War One and the Inter-War Years 1914–1939

THE OUTBREAK of the First World War had inevitably a devastating effect on British society and the Colony was no exception. One immediate effect was the arrival of wounded soldiers, including some from Belgium, who came to Hadleigh to convalesce.

The success of the Hadleigh scheme had relied very heavily on the very generous ratio of supervisory staff to the number of colonists. The 'Call to Arms' in 1914 reduced the pool of men from which those staff could be drawn. The introduction of conscription in 1916 exacerbated the problem, made even worse at the end of the war by the huge number of casualties. Throughout the country many of the great estates of Edwardian Britain lost the men without whose labour their very existence was threatened. Hadleigh Colony could not expect to escape these dramatic consequences.

A programme of retrenchment and revision was put in place, including the sale of much of the land bought at the beginning of the scheme. Most of the land sold was not in Hadleigh but in neighbouring Leigh-on-Sea. These were the farms bought by William Booth in 1892 and 1893 when the initial three Hadleigh farms proved insufficient for the General's ambitious plans. Leigh Park Farm, which had become the receiving centre for the colonists before they moved to the main part of the Colony, was sold in the 1920s to a Mr Walker who began the construction of what became the Highlands estate. The buyers were no doubt pleased to find they had inherited mature fruit trees from the Colony's orchards but perhaps rather less pleased and even

109. Leigh Heath Court. Built on the site of Leigh Heath Farm (*top*), one of a number of farms bought in Leigh-on-Sea when the Colony was expanded, but sold off in the 1920s and 1930s.

110. Florence Gardens, named after Bramwell Booth's wife, seen here under construction in the early 1920s (*top*) with the road still to be made up. The above picture shows bomb damage to the bungalows in the Second World War, June 1940. In 1986 to the east and south there was further construction of detached houses.

mystified by one of the clauses contained in the deeds of purchase: 'Neither the land nor any existing or future building thereon shall be used for the manufacture, sale or supply of wine, beer, spirits or other intoxicating liquors.' Leigh Heath farm to the south of the London road was sold in the 1920s and early 1930s to developers who built what is now known as the Marine Estate. Land south of the railway, including Two Tree Island and Leigh marshes was bought by Southend Corporation. The result of all these transactions was to confine the Colony to land in Hadleigh, very much the amount of land which remains today. Even in Hadleigh some land was sold, partly to widen the London road, but also for building. During the 1920s, 25 bungalows were built on former farmland to house retired Salvation Army officers and were named Florence Gardens after the wife of the Army's second General, Bramwell Booth. A recent review, published by Essex County Council, describes this exercise in social housing as 'a planned estate comparatively rare, particularly in Essex.' The bungalows, although no longer lived in exclusively by retired officers, have been part of a Conservation Area since 1997.

A guide to the Colony published at about the same time as the bungalows were built shows that despite the land sales most of the pre-war activities were continuing. The various departments still had their Superintendents; shire horses were still being bred and the 200 acres of market garden with its 10,000 fruit trees still sent its produce to Southend market as well as to Covent Garden. Most of the original buildings survived and some new ones had been added.

Religious activities were centred on the Citadel, the first building of significance a colonist would see as he came down Castle Lane. The building seated 500 and was used regularly for Saturday evening musical evenings as well as Sunday services. The Citadel corps included a band and a songster brigade as well as the home league, a weekly meeting for ladies. The young people's corps also had its own band as well as the sunbeams and life saving guards, The

111. The Citadel ceased to function in 1969 with the last service for the retirement of farm manager Lieut-Colonel Joseph Smith, and the final closure of the Colony Corps.

Salvation Army equivalent at that time of brownies and guides. The senior band was a regular participant at the Army Congresses at the Crystal Palace in South London where Colonel Brindley Boon recalled their appearance in 1925, its farm workers' smocks and cowboy hats being greeted with great enthusiasm.

112. The Colony Band prepares to depart for the celebrations at the Crystal Palace 1925.

113. Diamond Jubilee celebrations of The Salvation Army in 1925 took place at the Crystal Palace. Here we see a rehearsal in the colony grounds for the 'Grand March Past and Review.'

THE SALVATION ARMY,
LAND AND INDUSTRIAL COLONY.
HADLEIGH - - - - ESSEX.

A Grand . .
Variety Night
On
Wednesday, May 1st, 1935,
at 7-30 p.m.

By some of the Army's most Talented Artistes.

Adj. EVA FOURACRE (Gold Medallist) - Soprano.
S Ldr. M. C. ROBERTS - - - - Tenor.
D.B.M. T. GILES - - - - - Cornet.
S Bdsn. GEO. REED, L.R.A.M. - Piano Accordian.
Bdsn. PHIL. BARKER - - - Xylophone
Bdsn. R. DEBONNAIR - - - Recitals.

Chairman— THE GOVERNOR.
(Commissioner J. ALLISTER SMITH, O.F.)

S Bdsn. GEO. REED, L.R.A.M. - Accompanist.

Proceeds in Aid of Y.P. Band Instruments.

Programme . . . . Fourpence.

114. Variety Night programme giving an idea of the many musical evenings in the Colony Citadel. This programme was in aid of the Young People's Band, one of the many groups which flourished in the Colony Corps.

115. Spa Road London, scene of an open-air by the colony band.

116. Colony Citadel wedding group from June 1935 of Ralph and Edith Snow. Ralph Snow became the Bandmaster of the Temple band in 1938. Bandmaster George Watson is standing far right. Behind the bride and groom are Major W. Stewart, Major Wyman and Commissioner Allister Smith.

117. Boy Farmers for New Zealand sailing on the *ss Corintha*.

Two groups of boy farmers *en route* to New Zealand; the journey from Hadleigh to the port meant passing through the London main line railway stations.

118. Boy Farmers for New Zealand sailing on the *ss Tamaroa* September 1926. One of the boys was Eddie Cakebread, whose story is told in the Appendices.

LAND AND INDUSTRIAL COLONY, HADLEIGH, ESSEX

SCHEDULE of SERGT MAJOR ASHLIN's duties.

Boys' Emigration

Hours:	
5.45.a.m. till 7.15.a.m.	Dormitories & Dining Hall.
9.aM till 12.pm.	General duties in connection with the cleanliness of the Dormitories, Sergeant's Cubicles, Bath-house, Lecture Rooms, Store Rooms, Dining Hall etc.
12.pm till 12.45 pm	Dining Hall. See that everything is in order for dinner and discipline maintained.
	Parade boys for duty outside Dining Hall at 12.45.pm
2.15 till 5.pm	General duties.
5 pm till 5.45 pm	Dining Hall. Tea Time.
7.30 pm till 9 pm.	General walk round. See that all Sergeants are on duty at places appointed, taking care that one is always on duty in the Recreation Room, one in the Village, one at the Castle, one round Dormitories and Recreation fields, changing their duties each week.
Saturday afternoon.	Take a general walk round and see that all is O.K., making sure that the Sergeants are at their appointed places, as each one must be on duty on Saturday afternoon.
	Visit Dining Hall for Tea. See that all boys are on parade at 7 pm for the meeting. Endeavour to maintain discipline in all the meetings.
Sunday.	See that all the lads are up to breakfast by 8 am. Visit Dormitories after breakfast. See that all beds are properly made and Dormitories clean.

LAND AND INDUSTRIAL COLONY, HADLEIGH. ESSEX

= 2 =

Sunday. 10.30.am	See that all boys are on parade at 10.30 for morning meeting. Visit Dining Hall for dinner. General walk round in afternoon, seeing that all Sergeants are on duty.
	Visit Dining Hall for tea.
6.p.m.	Parade Boys at 6.p.m. for meeting.
	See that all boys are in Dormitories each night before leaving, and report on any bad conduct.

1/9/27

119. The schedule of a Sergeant-Major's duties gives a good idea of the daily routine on the Colony.

120. The ages of those shown here suggests this group was also part of the Boys Training Scheme in the inter-war years. Preparing for one of the many tasks undertaken by the teenage trainees.

121. Boy Farmers for Canada. Canada was a preferred destination as it was a much shorter and cheaper route for those emigrating.

122. Boy Farmers for Canada with numbers written on this old photograph from an attempt to identify all the lads. Note the same officer is accompanying this trip.

123. In training for departure to Australia, October 1926.

124. This picture shows how many of the boys were at the younger end of the age range.

125. General Bramwell Booth says farewell to a party of emigrants bound for Australia.

The most important innovation in the inter-war years was the Boys' Training Scheme. This included teenage boys between 14 and 19 who were to be trained to work in the Dominions overseas. William Booth's original scheme had envisaged an Overseas Colony to complement the City Colony and the Farm Colony. However, a lack of co-operation from the colonial governments meant this part of the Darkest England Scheme never worked as Booth had hoped. By the 1920s the Army was well established in countries such as Canada, Australia and New Zealand and even had its own local training schemes similar to Hadleigh to ensure a smooth transition from the Mother Country. By the mid 1920s some 3,000 boys had passed through Hadleigh. During their six weeks there they were instructed in the management of cattle, horses, pigs, milking, market gardening and fruit cultivation. They were also taught boot repair, rough carpentry, the cooking of 'homely dishes', washing underclothes and 'other domestic crafts which a lonely bachelor may find useful in isolated parts where his lot may be cast overseas.'

Lectures on farming were given by the Principal and lecturers of the East Anglian Institute of Agriculture. The boys lived in dormitories under the care of two officers and were offered opportunities for bowls, cricket, football and tennis. There was a recreation room with 'a library of wholesome literature' and various indoor games. Meals were served in their own dining room which today houses the Training Centre; the only surviving building, apart from a few houses, from this period of the Farm Colony.

126. Head Office in the main street of the Colony after it was moved from the end of Park Chase.

The Governor worked from Head Office which by the 1920s had moved from its original site at the junction of Park Chase and the London Road to Castle Avenue. Head Office, complete with its religious texts and a clock reminding all who passed by that 'Every hour should be for Jesus' was now in the centre of the Colony. The Home Office, the first building that any new arrival would see as he turned from Castle Lane into the Avenue, was responsible for the men's physical welfare. Superintendents still looked after the farm department, divided into the three sections; general farming, dairy and piggery, as well as the market garden, nursery and the brickfield. By this time, however, only brickfield three close to Sayer's farm remained in use. Brickfields one and two close to the main London Southend railway line had closed down.

In the early days of the boys' migration scheme Canada was the favoured destination but by 1927 the Army had chartered the *ss Vedic* to take 600 emigrants to Australia, a third being 'Hadleigh boys.' The Australian *War Cry* of that year records that the 200 boys from Hadleigh were received initially at the Mansion house in London, by the Lord Mayor, the Australian High Commisssioner, General Bramwell Booth and other Salvation Army officers. Seventy-five percent of the boys had trades, the rest were unemployed. This group was the latest of the 3,500 boys

127. ss Vedic. One of many ships assisting those who wanted to emigrate to Australia. This ship made four such trips. Here the ship is seen being welcomed by a Salvation Army band in Freemantle.

the Army had already sent to the dominions, themselves part of the 200,000 emigrants assisted by The Salvation Army's Migration Department. In more recent times emigration schemes arranged by organisations such as the Army have come in for their fair share of criticism, but at this time the Army claimed its failure rate was no more than one per cent.

During the voyage of the *Vedic*, described in great detail in the article in the Australian *War Cry*, some of the boys had helped the stokers while others had assisted the ship's butcher, baker and stewards. The *Vedic* was also carrying 300 young women destined for domestic service, and several of these became engaged to be married to some of the lads during the voyage. Some of these even wanted to get married on board ship but were told by Commissioner Unsworth, the Army officer in charge, that they must wait 'until they had made good in their jobs.'

Arthur Copping, who was reporting on the voyage for the Army's own journals, described what the crossing of the equator ceremony was like on a

128. 'Canaan' Riverview Training Farm for boys in Queensland was well established before 1900, as was Bayswater in Victoria. The purpose was not to cater for immigrant boys but for the needy and reformatory boys. Hadleigh boys, however, would have been placed here while in transition, until their placements were carried out.

129. Commisioner Henry, assisted by two officers greets new arrivals from Hadleigh Farm Colony in 1939. They arrived on the *ss Jervis Bay*, one of the last groups to sail before the outbreak of the Second World War.

130. New arrivals in 1921 on the *ss Zealandic*.

131. Melbourne City Temple c.1928. A welcome meeting for young men and women recently arrived on the *ss Vedic*.

132. Commander Herbert Booth on horseback, supervising the establishment of Riverview Boys Home.

133. The Colony Home League, a ladies meeting.

134. Home League outing c.1930. Westcliff Bus Company vehicle at the colony ready to depart. Commissioner Allister Smith is far right.

135. Hadleigh Colony Scouts, c. 1920s.

136. The Life-Saving Guards, c. 1924. The Salvation Army name for girl guides.

137. The Colony Band 1936 with Bandmaster George Watson seated behind the drum and Major W. Stewart, band trainer.

138. The Colony Songster Brigade c. 1925. Governor Commissioner Cuthbert.

139. The Colony Band taken at the Castle which at this time belonged to The Salvation Army.

140. Looking smart in their red tunics, the Colony band before the Second World War. In the middle row centre are left to right, Major W. Stewart, Commissioner Allister Smith, Major Wyman (Commanding Officer at the Colony) and Bandmaster George Watson.

141. Junior band in 1920 on an outing to Hockley Woods. Adjutant Greaves is standing far left.

142. A few of the Junior band boys standing behind the head office at the Colony. Note the bell in position above the building.

143. The school building can be seen behind these two bandsmen on the corner of Seaview Terrace. Frank Parsons holding his trombone and Ralph Snow.

'teetotal' ship. 'For four days before and after, the tuck shop sold 600 bottles of lemonade and ginger beer daily. By Act of Parliament each passenger was allowed four quarts (one gallon) of water each day. On this voyage the consumption of twelve gallons per person was causing the ship's captain no little anxiety.' After calling at Melbourne the *Vedic* sailed for Sydney with the New South Wales and Queensland emigrants, the latter group including 40 boys going to the Riverview Training Farm.

144. Boys in Training *c.*1926 photographed here outside the colony head office with Colonel Cuthbert and Commissioner Kitching

The Boys' Training and Migration Scheme continued through the 1920s and 1930s up to the outbreak of war in 1939. In April of that year 34 boys were still in residence at Hadleigh, twenty two of whom were due to sail later that month on the *S.S. Oronsay*. More had been notified to report for training, but as soon as war was declared on the third of September the Army's Migration Department said that all boys still in residence should be returned to their homes. The scheme was effectively at its end.

Some few years previously another group of young people had arrived on the Colony. On the outbreak of the Spanish Civil War in 1936 the British government had agreed to look after a number of Basque refugee children. Some of these came under the Army's care at the Clapton Congress Hall in East London and others came to Hadleigh. A young Salvationist named Brindley Boon was asked to organise games and entertainment each Saturday. These included football, cricket and an evening concert. He was assisted by Stanley Cottrell, and George Fuller, the Bandmaster of the International Staff Band.

More refugees arrived in 1939. Early in April, 30 Jewish refugees fleeing from Germany and Eastern Europe arrived in Hadleigh, and by the middle of May nearly 70 were living there, many of them in the dormitory accommodation in West View. The military authorities who had begun to requisition parts of the Colony on the outbreak of war, said because of the close proximity of the guns and searchlights, which they had installed, it would be impossible for the refugees to remain. So they returned to London.

One other event which was to have a considerable impact on the religious life of the Colony was the opening of the Hadleigh Temple corps in the High Street. The journey down Castle Lane to the Colony Citadel was becoming a problem for those Hadleigh Salvationists who didn't live on the Colony land. This was particularly true for the retired officers who lived in the Florence Gardens bungalows. The proposal to open a second Salvation Army meeting place in Hadleigh was not without its difficulties and presented a number of people with divided loyalties. Some felt if the building of the Temple went ahead the days of the Colony corps would be numbered. Despite these misgivings the Temple corps opened in January 1938. Today only one corps exists in

145. Brigadier Hugh Muir served the Colony as manager from 1936–1943. During his tenure, which saw the outbreak of the second world war, the Colony provided a haven for some sixty Spanish young people, who were refugees from the Spanish Civil War who arrived at the Colony in May 1937.

Hadleigh and the 1938 building has been replaced by the impressive structure designed by a local Salvation Army architect, David Greenwood.

If the outbreak of the First World War in 1914 forced the Colony to reconsider some of its original ideas including the sale of much of its land, then the coming of the Second World War was to have equally significant consequences.

146. Built by L. Upson & Son, and opened in January 1938. Hadleigh Temple Corps buildings.

147. The new Hadleigh Temple, designed by David Greenwood, and built on the same site as its predecessor above, was opened in February 2003.

World War Two and Post-War Re-adjustment 1939-1959

THE MOST far-reaching impact of the Second World War on the Colony was undoubtedly the arrival of the military authorities. The Thames estuary was clearly in the front line as far as the expected German air raids were concerned, hence the arrival of the guns and searchlights. The gun emplacement, close to Sayer's Farm, meant the closure of the one remaining brickfield. This was also the site of a major Army camp, and some of the farm buildings were used by the Royal Corps of Signals for their carrier pigeon service. Today the site is scheduled as an Ancient Monument. The military presence did bring some benefits; for example the army installed electricity in

148. Cattle herd making their way towards the World War Two gun emplacement which still remains near Sayer's Farm.

Sayer's farmhouse while they were doing the same in their own camp. This prompted The Salvation Army to enquire as to the cost of putting it into the nearby dairy which was done before the end of the year.

The Government exercised its wartime powers in other ways. By the end of 1939, 20 acres of grassland were ploughed for spring corn in order to increase the food supply. Although The Salvation Army's own Boys' Migration Scheme had now ended, it was approached by the Government to take boys for training in agriculture and market gardening under the scheme set up by Lord Derby. The Colony also received applications for some of the farmland to be turned over to allotments. Then, as if the encroachment of the military was not enough to deal with, an outbreak of swine fever in March 1940 meant the loss of 300 pigs. This same summer the Hadleigh Temple building in the High Street and some of the Florence Gardens bungalows were damaged in an air raid and all Salvation Army meetings were held in the Colony Citadel. Over 20 high explosive and incendiary

149. Opened on 8 January 1938, but just 18 months later in June 1940 the Hadleigh Temple building was badly damaged during an air raid.

bombs fell on the marshes; fortunately none of the livestock or buildings was damaged. A further problem was the closure of local markets due to the evacuation of much of the population of Southend and district. Although new markets were found in Wickford, Upminster and London these were not so profitable, made even less so since transport costs were now doubled because of the petrol shortage. Because of concern for the safety of livestock as well as Colony staff The Salvation Army had bought Potash Farm in Puttenham near Tring in Hertfordshire in order to evacuate the cattle including the dairy herd. By August 1940 nearly 60 cows had already been moved, although the dairy herd remained.

In order to meet the great demand for bricks the Government had appointed a 'Brick Director'. The Colony had 400,000 bricks remaining after the closure of the brickyard. The Salvation Army's Finance Council decided to reopen the brickfield 'as soon as weather permits.' This meant retaining the services of as many colonists as possible. Then at the beginning of 1941 the chairman of the Essex War Agricultural Committee asked for the dairy herd to remain at Hadleigh. The Government had now decided that the immediate threat of invasion had passed. In addition many people were now returning to Hadleigh and the surrounding area during this time that came to be known as 'the phoney war'. The Salvation Army agreed to the dairy herd remaining. By now the military had requisitioned not merely much of the land, but also many of the Colony buildings. These included most of the dormitory huts, the wash-house, lavatories, men's dining room and the shepherd's cottage on the Saddleback. This left the Colony with much reduced accommodation and severely restricted its farming operations. One area which expanded was the herd of grazing cattle: 50 more were bought in March 1942 and two months later that number was doubled. Labour shortages however continued to affect the running of the farm and in August the brickfield was once again closed.

An incident in June 1944 illustrated the problems caused by the military presence on Colony land. A fire broke out in the shepherd's cottage during the Army's manoeuvres; explosives were stored inside and the result was to leave the building a total ruin. It was never rebuilt. Today no trace remains of a place that many local people remember with great affection, particularly the friendliness of Mr Wanstell the shepherd.

150. A popular walk is across the saddleback from Hadleigh Castle towards Leigh-on-Sea. Along this route would have been the shepherd's cottage.

When the war ended in 1945 the Ministry of Works once again put pressure on the Colony management to reopen the brickworks to help with post-war reconstruction. In October 1945 Lieut-Colonel Wright was appointed manager in place of Brigadier Stewart who had been at the Colony since 1933. Brigadier Stewart left to take charge of The Salvation Army's International Staff Band. Some indication of the effects of the war and in particular the military occupation may be gauged from the decision taken in March 1946 to pull down the recreation room and number one dormitory because of their poor condition. The maintenance of the Colony's buildings was a constant headache to the management and a persistent drain on its finances. After 1945 the number of colonists continued to dwindle and The Salvation Army was faced with the problem of how it would make the best use of the 1,000 acres it still owned in Hadleigh. For a number of years arrangements were made with the Probation Service to take boys who had come before the courts. However this experiment did not last long as it required a high staffing ratio, so it ended in 1952. In June 1946 brickmaking was recommenced after the appointment of Mr Vivian as the brickfield superintendent. The main problem facing him was that most of the machinery was clearly obsolete and in need of replacement. Later that year Colonel Chard replaced Colonel Wright as manager.

151. Front cover of the 1947 National Music Camp brochure.

An entry in the Finance Council's minutes for March 1947 suggested to The Salvation Army's National Headquarters that a charge of ten shillings a head per week should be made for the use of the dormitory huts. In August of that year the Colony was 'invaded' by 98 young Salvationist musicians and their staff who formed the first boys' music camp to be held in the British Territory. The roll call of the staff and tutors reads like a Who's Who of well-known Salvation Army names from those immediate post-war years. The camp's Musical Director was Major E.V. Saywell, the National Secretary for Bands. The National Young People's Secretary, Brigadier Kaare Westergaard, was the Camp Director. They were assisted by Major George Smith, Adjutant Ernest Denham, Adjutant Charles Skinner, Adjutant D. Rolls, Major Ernest Rance, Band Instructor Ray Allen and Young People's Band

152. Band members assemble for a photo on the Colony.

Leader Herbert Osgood. Visitors to the camp included Commissioner John J. Allan, the Chief of the Staff, Commissioner William Dalziel, the British Commissioner, and Lieut-Colonel Bramwell Coles, the Head of the Music Department. Commissioner Allan had pioneered the first Salvation Army band camp in America as early as 1921 and Ray Allen (now Lieut-Colonel Ray Steadman-Allen) wrote the camp march appropriately named *Hadleigh Camp*. The Americans already had their *Star Lake* march. The week concluded with a special weekend at the Regent Hall in London's West End, where Brigadier Westergaard who presided over the Saturday evening programme was at pains to point out that since not all the boys could be present the representative band included boys chosen from every musical grade. 'Any idea that merit had governed the choice of the band must not be entertained', he said. This was to put right an earlier suggestion in *The Musician* that only students reaching the highest level would be able to attend the Regent Hall weekend. Clearly any suggestions of elitism were to be challenged in this pioneer venture.

Band camps were to continue at Hadleigh for the next eight years with the exception of 1948. In that year the camp moved to RAF Kenley in Surrey, a former World War Two fighter base. The very basic accommodation at Hadleigh, especially the dormitories, had been far from ideal, and perhaps also the impact of 100 teenagers arriving on a working farm had been underestimated. Major George Smith, the Assistant National Young People's Secretary, had managed to persuade the Group Captain in charge of Kenley to accept the contingent of boys as potential RAF recruits. Major Smith however had apparently omitted to mention that the boys would be bringing brass instruments with them. The following year the camp returned to Hadleigh where it was to remain for the next seven years. An item in the minutes of the Finance Council of 1955 suggests why the camps eventually moved from Hadleigh. It appears that they were causing too many problems for the daily running of the farm. Yet those early days at Hadleigh began a tradition that has continued to the present time.

In general the amount of post-war repairs needed on the Colony, in particular the expense of maintaining the brickfield, continued to be a financial headache. New plant for the brickfield was estimated to cost £26,000, a large sum of money 60 years ago. There was also a serious labour shortage. Neither the local labour exchanges, nor German prisoners of war, nor men from the Polish Army who were due for demobilisation were able to help. At this time the Manager moved out of Park House into *Amatikulu* in Castle Road. Park House was converted into two flats in order to accommodate two families. In 1950 Lieut-Colonel Wainwright was welcomed as Manager in

153. The bungalow as it is today in Castle Road. It was previously occupied by the Colony Governor until sold privately. It still retains its original name *Amatikulu*.

154. A formal photograph of the band camp members, 1947.

155. In a more informal mood ready for games and recreation. Most of the officers named on page 71 can be seen in the centre of this picture.

156. Ready to march away to the open-air meeting. The Head Office can be seen on the right as well as the brick built barns.

157. The same view today but showing more modern barns.

158. Seven young bandsmen with Adjutant Douglas Rolls, an instructor, outside the Citadel, 1947.

159. Holidays with Play! is how the brochure portrays the band camp. Adjutant Richard E. Holz, Territorial Music Director in New York wrote: *We wish you the best for the first British Music Camp. It should be an outstanding feature in such a famous brass band country.*

160. A 60th reunion was held in July 2007 at Hadleigh Temple Corps for delegates who attended the first camp in 1947.

161. Chums, the Army name for cubs, enjoying games in the Colony grounds.

162. There were also tennis courts. Both these illustrations early 1930s.

163. Mr Hopgood with a prize shire horse *c.* 1950

164. Welcome home tea in the dining hall June 1946 for those who have been serving in His Majesty's Forces.

165. Eric Ball in 1953 conducting the massed songsters from the local Salvation Army corps, inside the Colony Citadel.

166. Colonel John Wainwright (*right*), Governor of the Colony, shaking hands with Commissioner Allen, c 1951

167. Cottages in Chapel Lane, leading to Sayer's Farm, seen here behind the Army band, were formerly used as the village workhouse. Major Tulloch is marching in front of the band with Corps Sergeant Major Sykes.

168. Home League garden party held in the Colony grounds in July 1937. Lady Mary Wellesley (granddaughter of the Duke of Wellington) seen here with Brigadier & Mrs Hugh Muir, she was a volunteer working with the Spanish refugees.

169. The colony was also the venue for youth camps as well as band camps as these two photos show c. 1948.

place of Colonel Chard. Despite its problems the Colony's livestock continued to win prizes at local agricultural shows. In July 1949 it had won first prize at the Rochford show for the best 'turn-out' of 'Horse, Harness and Wagon'. The horse was called SALIC Major, a Percheron born and bred on the Colony.

In the same year as Colonel Wainwright's appointment a Production Officer arrived at the Colony to oversee a programme of reorganisation. The number of horses was reduced, the Friesian bull was to be sold and one lorry instead of two was to do the Farm's deliveries. Another reminder of the original 'Darkest England' scheme disappeared when it was agreed to convert the colonists' laundry into an implement store.

THE SALVATION ARMY
LAND & INDUSTRIAL COLONY
THE CITADEL · CASTLE LANE · HADLEIGH

IN THE CHAIR :—
THE BRITISH COMMISSIONER
(Commissioner Wm. R. Dalziel)

At the Annual

Partnership Festival

Guest Conductor : S/Major E. Rance
(National Secretary for Bands)

Taking Part:—
SOUTHEND CITADEL BAND (A. TUFFIN)
LEIGH-ON-SEA BAND   (E. JONES)
HADLEIGH TEMPLE BAND (G. WATSON)
Mezzo-Soprano—Songster G. Maureen Nobson
(Canford)
Accompanist at Piano—Bandmaster BERNARD WIGGINS
(Great Wakering)

SUPPORTING
THE CHAIR:
        Bernard Braine, Esq., M.P.
        Colonel & Mrs. J. Wainwright
            and Colony Staff
        Lt.-Colonel & Mrs. W. Wolfman
            and D.H.Q. Staff
        Major & Mrs. Cecil Gadsden
        Commanding Officers (Temple)

PROGRAMME   SATURDAY,
ONE SHILLING   20th January, 1951
                            at 7 p.m.

170. The front cover of the 1951 programme of one of the first Annual Partnership Festivals of the three local corps bands.

Lieut-Colonel George Bell arrived in 1952 to take over from Colonel Wainwright just in time to discover that the rear portion of the Citadel was derelict and unusable. This included the officers' room, the band room and the toilets. In addition the two coke stoves, the Citadel's only form of heating, needed replacing. The Citadel was not only still being used for Sunday worship but was also the venue for regular partnership festivals between local bands and songster brigades. Many people still remember their journey to these down an unlit Castle Lane especially on cold and wet winter evenings. The united bands and songster brigades of Hadleigh Temple, Leigh-on-Sea and Southend Citadel were frequent visitors. The annual three-band festival in aid of the February Self-Denial Appeal became in effect a local band contest. Even if marks were not officially awarded they were certainly given out unofficially by each band's supporters.

Individual cubicle lighting was suggested for West View where the remaining colonists were living. This was to 'prevent the present dangerous practice of reading by candlelight.' But it was pointed out 'Such lighting should be controlled by a master switch.' Clearly there was to be no encouragement to burn the midnight oil.

In January 1953 the East coast of England was badly affected by severe flooding. Although neighbouring Canvey Island was worst affected with a serious loss of life, the Colony lands didn't escape. One hundred and sixty acres of grassland and nearly 30 arable were flooded, as well as a 120 acres on Two Tree Island, which at that time the Colony rented from Southend Corporation. A number of cattle were marooned for 24 hours but eventually brought to safety. Colony staff also helped with the evacuation of Canvey and provided blankets and mattresses. Two years later the raising of the sea walls to prevent a similar re-occurrence reduced the Colony's area of pasture.

171. Peter Howard, who was appointed to take charge of pigs and poultry in 1953.

172. George Watson
was commissioned bandmaster in 1922. He was acting superintendent at the colony in 1923 then superintendent of the Market Garden. He retired in 1961 and was also Bandmaster of the Hadleigh Temple band.

In December 1953 Peter Howard was appointed to take charge of the pigs and poultry. At that time the Farm Department was being run by Mr Jagg and the Market Garden by Mr Watson, although both were past retirement age. The Watson family had arrived on the Colony very soon after it opened around about 1895. Mr and Mrs Watson brought with them six children and a number of grandchildren, of whom the George Watson mentioned here was one. All the men were experienced brickmakers from Sittingbourne in Kent. Although they were not the only family to be recruited from there they were the only ones to remain at Hadleigh. George Watson was nine when he arrived and spent the whole of his working life on the Colony. He finally retired in 1961 at the age of 74. In addition to his work, first in the brickfield and then in the market garden, he served as the Bandmaster, both of the Colony band and later of the band at the Temple corps.

In February 1955 the Roman 'fort' was registered as an ancient monument. Having another ancient monument on its land in addition to the Castle was to prove a mixed blessing as Colonel Bell, the Manager, was to discover. Later that year The Salvation Army proposed to sell some of its land north of the A13 in Templewood Road, Hadleigh, formerly part of Templewood Farm. In the same year Mr Trappit, a property developer asked to lease a piece of land in order to build 'flatlets'. The Army's response was indicative of how at least some senior officers saw the future of the farm. Colonel Edgar Dibden, the Chief of the Staff when writing to the Army's Chancellor of the Exchequer, said 'Personally I see nothing against leasing the land, but I think you should be careful in allocating land for this purpose so that it would not lessen the value of the entire Colony which we will wish to dispose of in due time.' At the same time other people were showing interest in buying Colony land. The Methodist church in Chapel Lane wanted to build a residence for their minister, and Benfleet Council wanted to buy the land west of the Florence Gardens bungalows to build more bungalows for the elderly. In exchange they were willing to install lighting in Florence Gardens. The Army's Chancellor of the Exchequer replied to the Chief of Staff, 'We should do well to allow these negotiations to go forward.' The future of the Farm Colony by the end of the 1950s was looking very uncertain.

173. A Roman 'fort' is believed to be here in this field, near Sayer's Farm, looking north towards the new housing in the distance close to Florence Gardens.

CHAPTER FIVE

An Uncertain Future; the Era of Commercial Farming 1960-1989

IN 1960 COLONEL BELL farewelled, having been manager for eight and a half years. His farewell brief gives an interesting snapshot of the Colony at the beginning of the next decade. The few colonists who remained continued to come mainly from the courts through the probation service. Unfortunately most of the men offered to the Colony were felt to have either mental problems, to suffer from serious physical defects or to be too old for heavy farm work. In addition the lack of a responsible officer to look after the colonists was proving a considerable handicap. Although 16 acres of the farm had now been sold, the Army's attempt to sell the remainder met with a refusal by the relevant authorities. There were also difficulties in bringing back into full cultivation the land that had been requisitioned by the War Office. The attempt to modernise the brickfield had swallowed up a great deal of money and kept the Colony's finances in a state of near bankruptcy. The extent of the financial problems is underlined by an item in the Colonel's report, which states that when the Colony was especially strapped for cash, large amounts of power and telephone cable buried in the military gun sites and their camp were dug up and sold.

The decision to close the brickfield in March 1956 had not only saved the Colony money, it also brought about a change of name. Hadleigh was now a Farm Colony and no longer a Land and Industrial Colony. This brought to an end William Booth's aim to make the Colony more than just an agricultural training ground. Even this greatly reduced aim to run the Colony purely as a farm was becoming increasingly difficult to achieve. Although many of the original departments continued to operate, and usually paid their way, much of the land was proving very difficult to cultivate, particularly the steep hilly areas covered with scrubland.

The Colony corps continued to operate at this time, its numbers increased by some tenants of the Colony attending the Citadel corps

174. A wedding on the Colony when the Citadel was still in regular use.

instead of the Temple where they were soldiers. When corps activities were transferred to the Temple a ruling was introduced that Colony employees and their families should attend the Citadel as their first priority. Not all Temple corps officers were happy with this arrangement. The continuation of the Saturday evening concerts at the Citadel also caused tension. A singing brigade led by Senior-Major Barnes and a Women's Fellowship led by the Manager's wife continued to exist.

In order to ease the pressure on the limited labour force now available, some of the Colony land began to be rented out. Fifteen acres near Leigh-on-Sea station was used by a Mr Theobald for grazing. Other land near the station was let to Southend Corporation for allotments. More allotments could be found behind Tattersall Gardens where Mr Wiggins, a local builder and friend of The Salvation Army, also leased some land. Fortunately, a suggestion that the area around the gun site should be re-purchased from the Military and used as a housing estate came to nothing.

At this time access by the public to Colony land was not encouraged. Trespass by local youth, including damage to the now defunct brickworks, was a considerable headache to the Colony authorities. Requests to excavate the Roman

175. All that remains today of where the Colony's Reliance herd of dairy cattle were milked.

'fort' were opposed and caused ill feeling locally. Similarly, pressure by the local authority for The Salvation Army to provide car parking for visitors to the Castle was strongly resisted. The bottom of Castle Lane, just past the Colony entrance, was a notorious bottleneck for cars and on more than one occasion the Colony was asked to lend a tractor to pull a stranded motorist from a ditch. Some camping was allowed, however, although this was normally for organised groups, mainly from churches. Cross-country events were also permitted. However, the most unexpected concession to the general public was the permission granted for the motor-cycle scrambles. They were organised by the Southend and District Motor Cycle Club on the dairy pasture and created much local interest. The largest was on the Whitsun Bank Holiday Monday, with a similar event on August Bank holiday. They appeared to create few problems and the course was reckoned to be one of the best in the south of England. The substantial donation offered to the Colony no doubt helped to overcome any earlier misgivings about damage to the land. The income generated went to support the dairy.

The Colony tradition of receiving people from abroad continued under Colonel Bell's management with the arrival of some foreign students who came to work on the farm or in the nursery. They had to be paid as colonists otherwise much higher wages would have had to have been paid under terms laid down by the Agricultural Wages Board; a further indication perhaps, of the financial problems the Colony was experiencing.

Some time after Colonel Green had replaced Colonel Bell as manager, General Kitching visited the Colony. The report of that visit contains some interesting facts and figures about the Hadleigh farm early in 1961. Four superintendents remained, two of them, Mr Jagg and Mr Watson being in their seventies. The various departments employed 24 people and 17 colonists; two of whom had been at Hadleigh since the 1930s. There were 32 tenants still living on the Colony as well as a number of Colony pensioners living elsewhere. The total acreage of land was still over 900 acres. Cattle numbered over 150, pigs around 230 and poultry 400. Milk yield was nearly 36,000 gallons annually; much of it going locally to Howard's dairies.

An internal memorandum from International Headquarters three years later paints a less optimistic picture. One particular area of concern was the lack of use of the Penitent Form or Mercy Seat in the Citadel. Only one Salvation Army soldier had been made from those kneeling there in the past 15 years. Although six colonists had knelt there, one had apparently threatened the others with violence if they refused to come forward. He was now in Borstal. Concern was also expressed once again about the Colony's finances. In the nine years from 1955 to 1964 the farm had received nearly £89,000 in grants. Despite this assistance the figures for March 1964 revealed a deficit of over £2,000. Much needed expenditure on the reconstruction of the dairy, the modernisation of West View, where the colonists lived, and other refurbishment would cost up to £12,000.

A further issue at this time was the overall state of the Colony as The Salvation Army's Centenary Year approached. In 1965 the Army would celebrate 100 years since William Booth had taken charge of the East London Christian Mission. The name Salvation Army was not used officially until 1878. Many overseas visitors were expected in London for an international congress. They were certain to include many from Commonwealth countries such as Australia, Canada and New Zealand, places to which Hadleigh trainees, men and boys had travelled in search of a new life overseas. What they would expect to find at Hadleigh, it was believed, would be a model farm, not 'dilapidated sheds and huts which ought to be removed.' What was clear was that neither the staff nor the money was available to carry out the necessary restoration. That same memorandum from Headquarters asked the question 'Is this tremendous expenditure justified by the results?' Once again the issue of the Colony's purpose had been raised since it no longer appeared to be fulfilling its original aims. If it was still intended to retain the farm, since selling it for development did not appear to be an option, various proposals were put forward. These included building either an officers' convalescent home, a home for retired officers, flats or bungalows for retired officers or a children's home. None of these proposals ever came to anything, and by the mid-sixties the Army was left with a farm whose social purpose had all but disappeared.

176. Peter Howard with his son Paul, who succeeded his father as Farm Manager.

The person with the responsibility for the daily running of the farm from the autumn of 1962 was Peter Howard. Peter had arrived in Hadleigh in December 1953 to take charge of the pigs and poultry. He came from a farming background. His mother had employed land-girls, one of whom, Mildred, was to become Peter's wife. Peter and Mildred were to remain on the farm for the next thirty-nine and a half years. They were both very keen to maintain at least some part of William Booth's vision for the Colony, but at the same time Peter knew that he had to make the farm as viable a commercial proposition as possible.

In January 1963 Colonel Smith arrived as manager to take over from Colonel Green, and although he was due to retire in March 1968 he remained in the post for a further year. After Colonel Smith's retirement Peter officially took over as farm manager on 1 March 1969 the first non-officer to hold that position in the almost 80 years of the Colony's history. He became directly responsible to the Finance Secretary and the Chancellor of the Exchequer at International Headquarters. He was in charge when the Colony Citadel closed its doors for the last time in 1969. Albert Cotton, a former officer, had been in charge of its Sunday worship during its final months. At this time the farm still supported pigs, chickens, the market garden and the dairy with its 100 Friesian cows. There were between ten and twelve employees, though only one former colonist. However by 1973 the dairy-herd was experiencing feeding problems. Insufficient grass was a major cause, although staffing problems didn't help.

It was about this time that Essex County Council put forward plans to turn much of the area south of the London Road between Leigh and Benfleet into a country park. The Farm Colony sat right in the centre of this land that the County Council was prepared to buy. The Army, on the other hand, was more interested in selling off at least some of it's land to developers. A letter sent out from the Benfleet Urban District Council Offices in January 1973 stated that the Army had applied to the Council to develop 133 acres of Colony land for residential purposes. The Council itself was seeking to acquire some four acres of Colony land for residents. The same letter also spoke of the possible need for a relief road or by-pass through Hadleigh using Salvation Army land. The news of the proposed residential development prompted a response from the chairman of the Hadleigh Ratepayers' Association showing the area to be affected by the proposed development as well as where the relief road would be built. The Secretary of State for the Environment now became involved by announcing that a public enquiry would be held to look at all these applications. The Salvation Army was now very much in the local limelight but not for the reasons it would have wished.

The following year the Colony was once again in the local newspapers. After the Army's plans to sell land for housing had been rejected, Peter Howard, the farm manager, was left with the task of continuing to farm on a commercial basis. In order to do this he believed that much of the scrubland needed to be cleared to make the most effective use of the land. This brought him into conflict with local conservationists and environmentalists who believed this was destroying a natural habitat for wildlife. Similarly the Nature Conservancy was unhappy with a scheme to drain two hundred acres of marshland south of the railway. In the meantime Peter had other problems not related to farming policy. The hobby of collecting old bottles and jars had attracted a number of collectors to the Victorian debris which had lain on the Colony since its early days when sailing barges had brought cargoes of London's rubbish to construct the farm's railway embankments. As the number of these bottle hunters grew so did the problems they brought with them, including dangerous broken bottles and fragments of china left lying around. Many fences were also damaged.

Eventually the proposal to create a country park went ahead, but mainly on the land of an adjacent farm rather then that of the Colony. As far as the Colony farm was concerned the availability of various grants enabled a programme of rebuilding to take place. The initial grants came from the United Kingdom and then later from the European Economic Community. The Ministry of Agriculture put in place a Farming and Horticultural Development Scheme (FHDS). This enabled the marshland to be drained and a number of new buildings including barns, to be erected. The semi-derelict appearance of the Colony, a cause of so much concern in the mid 1960s, began to change. At the end of the '70s two new reservoirs were created. This allowed all the fields to be irrigated with main drains. Even the potato fields could be watered which meant a yield of between 1,200 and 1,500 tons a year could be maintained. The sign on the London Road advertising Salvation Army potatoes was a familiar sight to local people.

177. Built originally for the farm manager and his family, this building is shared at present as an administration centre by the Farm Manager and the Training Centre.

One of the greatest disappointments for Peter and Mildred, themselves soldiers of the Hadleigh Temple corps, was the failure of the Colony to continue as a major part of The Salvation Army's social outreach programme. Several small-scale schemes were tried at this time. A few alcoholics from the Booth House Social Centre in Whitechapel were brought down from London, and a detoxification unit was set up under the leadership of Kenneth Henderson. The group lived in West View although they later moved into Castle House, the original farmhouse, dating from 1709, until it was pulled down. In 1980 a new farmhouse was built for Peter and his family. This now

178. The Boys' Dining Room became the training centre when it was opened in 1990.

houses the administrative offices shared between the farm and the training centre.

Under privileged children from Salvation Army centres in Stratford and Deptford came for their summer holidays, staying in West View. In spite of the new buildings some physical evidence of the earlier Land and Industrial Colony still remained: principally the Citadel, the boys' dining room and West View. Although other domestic buildings such as Seaview Terrace and Mount Zion were still being used, the former three were not. In the late 1980s Peter Howard wrote to General Eva Burrows expressing his concern about the future of these buildings. The answer for at least one of these came in 1990, almost exactly a hundred years after William Booth's purchase of the three Hadleigh farms. The boys' dining hall was to become a new training centre. It seemed that at long last Booth's original vision for Hadleigh was about to be reborn.

179. A view from the entrance looking towards the houses along Seaview Terrace.

CHAPTER SIX

Hadleigh Training Centre and Farm 1990 to the Present

180. General Eva Burrows opening the new Hadleigh Training Centre on 7 September 1990.

MANY PEOPLE CONTRIBUTED to the idea of opening a new training centre on the site of the Colony farm. The official opening ceremony was conducted by General Eva Burrows on the seventh of September 1990 in the presence of Sir Bernard Braine, the local MP who was a good friend of The Salvation Army. The many other guests included members of the Booth family. The first officers in charge of the centre were Captains Alan and Sandra Ford. The centre itself was situated in the former boys' dining hall. The trainees of the 1990s would be those designated with special training needs rather than the 'down and outs' of Booth's original enterprise. The centre aimed to provide a programme that would help people between 16 and 55 with their personal development and enable them to realise their potential in mainstream education, training or employment. Its original departments concentrated on catering, carpentry and computing. The centre continued to grow under successive managers including Captains Peter and Janet Bale and Beverley Egan, who had been a staff member since the beginning and became the manager, serving in that post for ten years. Beverley went on to become the Divisional Director for Community and Social Services for the London North-East Division of The Salvation Army. As such, her involvement with the centre continued in her monitoring and support for the management team.

In December 2001 a new tearoom was opened at the rear of the training centre. Imaginatively designed by David Greenwood, then The Salvation Army's Chief Architect, it serves a number of purposes. First it offers the trainees an excellent opportunity to demonstrate their catering as well as retail skills when meeting and

181. On the terrace of the tea rooms, customers enjoying the sunshine and superb views across the estuary.

serving the public. Second it gives the public not only a place to enjoy refreshments in a welcoming atmosphere but also a chance to experience the training centre's aims at first hand. From its earliest days the management's policy has been to serve Fair Trade produce wherever possible. The centre is in a very popular area for walkers with public footpaths close by and the Castle within easy walking distance. A large car park also enables visitors who arrive by car easy access to the tearoom. The number of weekly visitors has now reached 2,500.

The present manager is Shelley Carter, previously Beverley Egan's deputy. Shelley is continuing the policy of extending the centre's programme. She is assisted by two deputy managers, Derek Bill and John Swann, as well as by 50 members of staff and 30 volunteers. John's story was recorded in an article in a local newspaper. 'Ten years ago John believed he was finished after an industrial accident left him with only limited use of his limbs. John, a former mechanic, lost his thriving garage business and all hope for the future.' The article continued by saying that even after two operations John's efforts to change his career ended in failure. He said ' I'd gone from making a decent active living with my hands to feeling like I was going to be left on the shelf.' His doctor then suggested that he start a 12 week course at the Hadleigh Training Centre. After completing the course John was offered a position as a centre tutor. He later became a deputy manager. He concluded 'This centre put me back on my feet and gave me a new start. I never realised before how important the name Salvation Army was. It was certainly my salvation.'

Training given at the centre is based on National Vocational Qualification standards (NVQs), and is under the personal direction of the tutors of each department. Many of the products of the carpentry department are on sale at the tearoom, and range from smaller items such as bird and insect boxes to garden benches and trellises. The Information Technology and Graphic Design department produces most of the training centre and tearoom's design requirements. A very popular department with the trainees is Office Skills, where teaching ranges from the very basic to the advanced. The Estates Management Department often has work commissioned from within the local community. It has its own workshop, has constructed an ice cream kiosk for the tearoom and sets up and monitors the monthly farmers' market.

182. Shelley Carter, the present manager at the Training Centre.

183. Working in the kitchen (*Left and below*)

Some of the opportunities offered to the trainees.

184. Workers inside the polytunnel.

185. Horticultural work, working with the trainees.

186. Field management. Workers hedge laying.

187. Workers, hedge planting.

188. Construction of a garden at the farm entrance.

189. New barns at the Colony farm.

190. Modern farm machinery.

191. Simon Gibson
with bull.

192. Pedigree Hereford bull and calf.

193. Free range chickens 2003.

194. Estates management (*above and right*).

195. Trainees working on the Rare Breeds Centre (*above and right*).

196. Reception – trainees from the IT department.

197. Shop in the tea rooms.

198. General John Gowans in the IT department on the occasion of his visit in 2000.

199. Working in the IT department.

200. Learning carpentry skills. Some of the work from this department has gone to the Little Havens Children's Hospice in Daws Heath.

201. Commissioner Alex Hughes, who at the time of his visit in 2000 was the Territorial Commander, seen here in the carpentry section.

202. General John Gowans unveiling the newly restored fountain at the entrance to the Colony with centre manager Beverley Egan, in 2000.

203. Joe Pike, chairman of Essex County Council (*third from left*) seen here with other guests including General John Gowans and centre manager Beverley Egan.

204. Architect David Greenwood talking with General Gowans, 2000.

205. Commissioner Alex Hughes looking at plans with David Greenwood.

206. The tearooms were opened by the Mayor of Castle Point, Councillor Liz Brett on 4 December 2001.

207. Lieut-Colonel David Phillips and Beverley Egan with the Mayor, who is unveiling a plaque – *so that the local community may enjoy God's creation.*

Hadleigh trainees were involved in the construction of the band stage within the successful Salvation Army garden, 'From Darkness to Light', and designed by Julian Dowle, shown at the Chelsea Flower Show in 2004. An even earlier project in 1996 by the woodwork tutor, Mark Groenenberg, and his trainees, was the construction of a footpath and footbridge in the Essex Wild Life Trust Nature Reserve in Pound Wood in nearby Daws Heath. This was to enable visitors to get a closer look at the bluebells for which the wood is famous. The Horticultural Department also makes use of the farmers' market as a regular outlet for its produce as well as providing a stall on the tearoom terrace. It is now providing produce for the tearoom itself, in this way reducing the number of food miles involved. A portakabin is used as a potting shed and a second polytunnel has now been added to the original one. Whereas many of the trainees remain in the centre, the Employment Development Department has been successful in arranging supported employment, paid work, work experience, voluntary work and mainstream college placements for a large number of trainees.

The first farmers' market, held in conjunction with the farm, took place in March 2003. Since then it has grown to become one of the busiest in the county; boasting over 20 regular stall-holders and a very large number of customers, stretching the car park facilities to the limit. The market is held every second Wednesday of each month except for January. It is now recognised as a certified farmers' market.

A great support to the centre manager, the staff, volunteers and trainees is the chaplain Heather Sheldon, a Salvationist from the Hadleigh Temple corps. The

208. A scene at the monthly Farmers Market.

first chaplain was Hilary Davison, who did much to remind those who work at the centre as well as those who visit the tearoom that the Training Centre is part of The Salvation Army's world-wide social and evangelistic work. Hilary was also actively involved in work to make the old dining hall and its surroundings ready for the new venture. Leigh-on-Sea corps, just a few miles away, had developed its own successful Manpower Community Services programme for the unemployed. Hilary was responsible for managing this programme in the Leigh-on-Sea Community Centre, and when the government closed the scheme, Hilary donated the workshop equipment, tools and materials to the new project at Hadleigh. Just as the Land and Industrial Colony won prizes for its produce and animals so the Training Centre has also won a number of awards. These include the Southend and District Business Award for the development of staff training, a similar award for community work, and the Essex Countryside Business Award, also for community work.

Today the work of the Training Centre continues the vision of William Booth, although it meets a very different kind of need from the one the original Land and Industrial Colony sought to address. Yet the modern day visitor to the tearoom may, with a touch of imagination, catch something of the spirit of that first social experiment which also attracted numerous visitors to see exactly what it was that the Army's founder had in mind for this corner of South East Essex.

While the Training Centre was being established in the former boys' dining hall Peter Howard continued his work as farm manager. In 1993 he retired, having worked on the Colony first as an employee, and then as farm manager, for almost 40 years. He was succeeded by his son Paul, already working with his father on the farm. Soon after taking over Paul was approached by Essex County Council who wished to purchase some land in order to make a car park in Chapel lane for visitors to the country park. The terms of their purchase included a promise not to use the land for 'the sale, supply, manufacture or advertising of wines, beers, spirits or any other intoxicating liquors, nor for any noxious or offensive trade or business, nor as betting shop, nor for gambling, nor as place for public dancing.' Even in 1993 the spirit of William Booth lived on in Hadleigh.

209. Simon Gibson with his wife and family. Simon is the current Farm Manager.

Today the farm, managed by Simon Gibson, comprises just over 800 acres, almost the same amount of land as the three farms bought by William Booth in 1891. Although the total area of the farm may be similar to that of 1891,

210. A view of the Citadel in 2000.

211. By 2003 the bulldozers had moved in to demolish the Citadel building.

212. The view from the fountain across to the tea rooms after the Citadel building had been completely demolished.

213. The same scene in October 2007 when the builders moved in to commence work on the new extension.

214. Work on the new extension in progress, February 2008.

it's doubtful whether the original colonists would recognise much produced on the farm today. Oilseed rape, beans and an area for organic crops including seed oats and wheat grown specifically for bread making may also be found. The farm is part of organic farming in the United Kingdom, which has more than doubled its area and output in recent years. This particular development reflects the farm's mission statement that says 'The Mission of Hadleigh Farm is to restore and enhance the local environment; to become a place where people can become informed, wildlife can flourish and by example profitable farming can be practised. To ensure that those we come into contact with are aware of and influenced by the values of The Salvation Army. To rekindle the place of dreams.'

215. Hereford cattle at the farm.

Animals are still to be found at Hadleigh but the cattle are now reared for beef as the dairy has long since closed. The beef herd is now entirely pedigree Herefords reared organically. A recent innovation, opened in 2004, is the Rare Breeds Centre managed by Ginny Gibson, Simon's wife. Here one will find a variety of breeds of pigs, sheep, goats and hens. This is open to the public through-out the year and attracts a large number of visitors, especially families. Two days of each week are currently given over to school visits. In 2006 the rare breeds centre attracted 40,000 visitors. Recent developments include a living willow maze, a wildlife garden and a wildflower meadow. The farm is also very much involved in the monthly farmers' markets, selling its organic beef and using its barns to offer accommodation to the stall-holders.

Simon Gibson, who became farm manager in July 2001, lives with his family in a farmhouse built as part of the Army's Millennium Project. This new bungalow at the end of Seaview Terrace is on the site of the Colony schoolroom. Simon has discovered that not only is he the custodian of a large slice of Salvation Army history and three ancient monuments, but also there is evidence of an even earlier period of settlement than that indicated by the presence of the Roman 'fort'. There is clear indication of the existence of Red Hills, which are the remains of Iron Age and Roman salt production sites once common along the Essex coast. Fragments of pre-Roman, Roman and Mediaeval pottery have also been found, indicating that the Hadleigh site has a long and important history of settlement. The area surrounding Park House is also believed to have been at one time a Royal Park where kings hunted.

216. Grey face Dartmoor rare breed lamb.

The farm is part of the Countryside Stewardship Scheme that encourages conservation and care for the environment alongside modern farming methods. Strips of land on the edges of fields are left

217. The Salvation Army had its own day school on the Colony, opened in 1903 which helped alleviate overcrowding in Hadleigh village. Major Collins was the headmaster. On the same site today is the new home for the Farm manager (*right*).

unploughed to encourage their use by wildlife. Also the ancient craft of hedge-laying is practised and this too encourages wild life.

Just as the opening of the Training Centre, the new Temple building on the London Road, and the tearoom were part of a new Salvation Army vision for Hadleigh, so the farm under Simon's management is also looking to the future. Some of the details of this new vision for the farm still remain to be realised, including the opening of a farm shop and a further extension of the Rare Breeds Centre. The Land and Industrial Colony built on the purchase of the original three farms might exist no longer but in its place is a farm which is clearly aiming to show how The Salvation Army today can be a good steward of God's earth.

October 2007 saw the beginning of a further chapter in the story of the Training Centre. Building began on phase one of a project to provide a new tea-room, a shop area and public toilets. This phase is due for completion in July or August 2008 Phase two will see a complete refurbishment of the Training Centre, due to be finished by November of the same year. These buildings are being constructed on the site of the former Citadel.

218. The proposed new Salvation Army Tea Room and Training Centre extension.

(Illustration courtesy of Ayshford Samsome Architects)

SALVATION ARMY COLONY

The Salvation Army bought the land
High above the Old Leigh strand.
The unemployed from London towns
Were brought by Booth to Hadleigh Downs,
To his new farm colony to learn a trade:
Save their souls? Have a new life made?

Down Castle Lane they built their farm
With accommodation to house the swarm
Of colonists that herded cows and sheep
Or laboured in the fields to earn their keep.

The Hadleigh villagers were opposed at first;
Destitute vagabonds! They feared the worst,
Fighting and thieving, stock would be lost.
The colony would close off paths that crossed
Their land, denying access to the nicer parts
Where locals picked berries for pies and tarts.

The plan developed; village fears came to nought.
Other trades as well as farming were taught:
Brickmaking, pottery and construction skills
Were learned by many on the riverside hills.

Today training continues in a number of ways
Farm produce is sold on monthly market days.
There is a rare breeds centre with visitor information
And a trainee run tearoom with a growing reputation.

Dominating the view the castle ruins stand bare
The colonists long gone but 'The Army' is still there.

Essex Man

Inspired by John Barr's poem in 'Darkest England' and published 2006 in
The Essex Hundred.

Appendices

Darkest England in Rochford Hundred

The Destiny of Hadleigh Castle

*A reporter from the local Southend Standard newspaper finally catches
up with Commissioner Elijah Cadman, the officer put in charge of Booth's scheme.*

INTERVIEW WITH Commissioner Elijah Cadman in the *Southend Standard* 23 April 1891

'The task set me on Monday – that of finding Mr Commissioner Cadman of The Salvation Army – was not easy of accomplishment, but by dint of perseverance during the afternoon I 'ran down' the gentleman I sought, and he kindly came down from the platform at Exeter Hall, where he was assisting to conduct a very large meeting.

We went to business without parley. 'I have come to ask you, sir' said I 'As to the farms you have taken for the social scheme of The Salvation Army near to Southend. We at Southend, as you may imagine, are very much interested in the fact that we are going to have the opportunity of seeing the working of such a great undertaking so close to us. When are you coming into possession?'

Cadman replied 'We can hardly say, because it's all a question of settlement'

SS 'Can you give me any general idea as to what will be done with the property?'

CC 'Well, we shall practically do just what it states in The 'Darkest England' book. The place will develop. We shall have a great deal of salvage and we shall put a few hundred people at work on the premises. A lot of small houses will be built, and we shall make a sort of little town of it. We intend to grow almost all our own consumption. We shall make our own bricks, have our own mills, and give people a thorough training for their future lives, bringing them from their poverty, and ultimately we shall be able to send some of them to the Colony over the sea.'

SS 'What about Hadleigh castle?'

CC 'We shall have pilgrimages to it. We shall be taking boatloads and trainloads to it, and we shall be making a very great deal of the neighbourhood. Of course there won't be the same freedom and rights as there have been, only by the ordinary road where the right of way is.'

SS 'Shall you issue tickets for viewing?'

CC 'Ordinary permits would be given for going over the farm, and people will get everything explained to them on the spot by officers in command of the different branches. Of course there will be lots of works and different manufactures.'

SS 'You won't charge anything for the permits?'

CC 'We will give them to any friends or anybody who wants to go over the buildings.'

SS 'Can you tell me in what way these farms are specially suited to your requirements?'

CC 'One reason is that we have got half a mile abutting on the water; where we can, as we propose to do, put up landing stages and wharves, and we shall use the water more than the railway for carrying purposes. Besides, it is a very healthy place, and we have there a heavy land, a moderate land, and a light land.'

SS 'Will the castle be put to any use?'

CC 'Oh yes; we shall put it to a variety of uses and we shall make it as interesting as possible.'

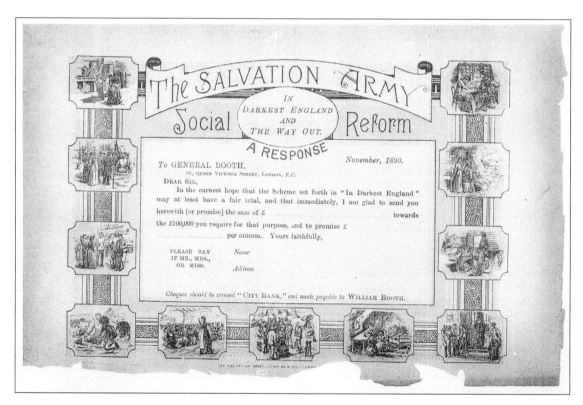

219. An indication of how William Booth's Darkest England Scheme was to be financed.

The Salvation Army Land and Industrial Colony
Hadleigh, Essex

List of Governors and Managers – as far as is known.

Harold Moore	1891	Consulting Director, non-Salvationist from Colchester
Major Wright	1891	Governor
Commissioner Elijah Cadman	1895	Governor
Colonel David C. Lamb	1898	Governor
Colonel John B. Laurie	1910	Governor
Colonel Wilfred Simpson	1915–1916	Governor
Colonel Isaac Unsworth	1917–1918	Governor
Colonel W. Samuel Stitt	1919–1921	Governor
Colonel George Jolliffe	1922–1924	Governor
Colonel David Cuthbert	1925–1929	Governor
Commissioner J. Allister Smith	1930–1936	Governor
Brigadier Hugh P. Muir	1937–1943	Manager
Lieut-Colonel Hector Wright	1943–1946	Manager
Colonel John Wainwright	1949–1952	Manager
Colonel George Bell	1953–1959	Manager
Colonel Charles Green	1959–1962	Manager
Lieut-Colonel Joseph Smith	1963–1969	Manager
Peter Howard	1969–	Manager

PROPERTY PURCHASED BY WILLIAM BOOTH IN HADLEIGH AND LEIGH-ON-SEA

HADLEIGH HOUSE (later Victoria House)

At one time lived in by Lady Nicholson and later purchased by The Salvation Army. Licensed as a voluntary retreat under the Inebriates Acts of 1879, 1899. Opened in 1901. Inmates paid 20/- (twenty shillings) per week for treatment. At one time had warehouse in basement. Accommodation for 25 men.

HADLEIGH HALL

The Salvation Army purchased part of Hadleigh Hall Estate and William Booth purchased this house c. 1899. In the early 1900s the property became the Governor's Residence. Sold/leased to Dr James in 1937 who opened a surgery with Dr Sam McGladdery

THE HOMESTEAD (formerly Blossoms)

Purchased by The Salvation Army who renamed it 'The Homestead'. It housed colony employees. Abandoned during WW1 and demolished in the 1920s

CASTLE FARM

Purchased by The Salvation Army in 1891, built in 1706 on the site of an earlier house. It was demolished in the 1970s

SAYER'S FARM

Original owner believed to have been William Sayer as far back as 1491. Present building dates back to 1810. Current residents are Mr and Mrs B. R. Bull.

PARK FARM

Part of Castle Park, a royal hunting area – Medieval. Probably unofficial Hotel. Re-built by Lady Olivia Sparrow c. 1861. Purchased by The Salvation Army in 1891 from Major Thomas Jenner Spitty, area known as Hadleigh Park. Bed and Breakfast provided by Superintendent's wife. Later became Governor's residence. Afterwards divided into two flats. Unoccupied at the present time.

LEIGH PARK FARM

Around 67 acres c. 1850. Purchased by The Salvation Army c. 1893 and later sold to Mr Walker in the 1920s. The remaining two cottages in Olive Avenue are now part of the Highlands Estate.

BELTON HILL FARM, LEIGH

Purchased in 1891 to allow easier access from the Colony to the railway station, at that time in its original situation in the village of Leigh.

TEMPLEWOOD FARM, HADLEIGH

Situated north of the London Road. Also purchased in the 1890s and later sold.

LEIGH HEATH FARM

185 acres *c.* 1850. Purchased by The Salvation Army in 1893 from William Stewart Forster and William Cholmeley for £5,500. In June 1927 The Salvation Army sold eastern part to Southend-on-Sea Estates Company for £17,000. The Salvation Army paid half the cost for the construction of Thames Drive. Now part of the Marine Estate.

LEIGH MARSH FARM

The Salvation Army purchased Farm and Fishery in 1892 from William Foster. Sold to Southend Corporation in 1936.

VINE COTTAGE

High Street, Hadleigh. Was occupied by Market Garden employees. Now a preserved building.

COMPTON

Original Head Office on the corner of Park Chase and later became employee accommodation.

HILLCREST

A bungalow, near to Park Farm, also used as employees' accommodation. Neither 'Compton' nor 'Hillcrest' exists today.

New Zealand
IMMIGRATION
FARM TRAINING SCHEME
1924-1930

The New Zealand *War Cry* references to immigration, especially groups of young men who came under The Salvation Army Farm Training and Employment Scheme do not mention individuals by name. However, shipping lists are available at the New Zealand National Archives. Here is some of the information recorded in the NZ *War Cry*.

SHIP: SS REMUERA

Arrived: Wellington 3 November 1924

9 Boys aged 14–19 years of age, all Boy Scouts from the 1st Crowborough Troop, Crowborough, Sussex, arrived with Scoutmaster F.G. Southon, having undergone agricultural instruction for 18 months at Hadleigh Farm. They were sent to farms at Kaeo, Matamata, Ohingaiti, Morrinsville and Whangarei.

SHIP: SS ATHENIC

36 lads Arrived Auckland on 24 November 1924. Captain Charles Liddell aged 45 was the conductor.

SHIP: SS IONIC

Arrived: Wellington 19 February 1925

38 young men arrived with Brother Elliott from Falkirk, Scotland, who acted as chaplain for the voyage. They proceeded to farm positions secured in advance.

SHIP: SS CORINTHIC

Arrived: 15 May 1925

47 youths arrived and proceeded to Putaruru Training Farm. Major G. Stone was the conductor.

22 August 1925

'A Visitor from England' article tells of Lieut-Colonel W. Powell speaking about unemployment in England and the opportunities available in New Zealand and The Putaruru Farm Training Scheme.

SHIP: SS CORINTHIC

Arrived: Wellington 23 October 1925

53 young men arrived and proceeded to positions in farm work having had previous training at Hadleigh Farm, where some had been converted and enrolled

as soldiers of The Salvation Army. Major Hector Wright was their conductor, from The Salvation Army Migration Headquarters in Montreal Canada. His visit was to help establish the Immigration Department along the lines similar to Canada, with an emphasis on *wise distribution* and *aftercare*. He spoke of the 1917 visit of Lieut-Colonel Fudge, now the Inspector of Immigration Affairs with THQ Montreal and the 'interests of after war emigration'

26 January 1926
Visit to New Zealand of Commissioner and Mrs David Lamb is recorded.
A great number, but not all migrants came from a rural population. The Salvation Army code of standards for selection were *Healthy and enterprising boys* and *a Spirit of self-reliance and independence.* Initial training at Hadleigh farm and situations provided for the boys on arrival.
Many remained under Salvation Army guardianship until the age of 21.

SHIP: SS ATHENIC
Arrived: Auckland 13 March 1926
44 young men aged 17–19 arrived and Brother Joseph Hay was their conductor, aged 38. They proceeded to Putaruru for training. It is noted that so far 218 lads have come to New Zealand under General Booth's migration scheme.

6 November 1926
Photograph in the War Cry of officers of the Immigration Department at THQ, Wellington. Ensign Toomer (Auckland), Captain Sansom (Wellington), Major Greene (Resident Secretary) and Commandant Middlemiss (After Care Officer).

SHIP: SS TAINUI
Arrived: Wellington 14 November 1926
22 lads arrived with Bandsman Ernest Coxhead of Southend 1 Corps in England in charge. They were sent to Putaruru for three months training.

SHIP: SS TAMAROA
Arrived: Wellington 25 July 1927
38 young men arrived and sent on to farm situations in the North Island. Envoy A. Noakes was the conductor.

SHIP: SS CORINTHIC
Arrived: Wellington 25 October 1927
It is recorded that shortly after their arrival this party of lads were met by the Commissioner (no name) who gave helpful counsel and prayed with them. W. Stubbington, a Salvation Army Bandsman was the conductor.

SHIP: SS TAINUI
Arrived: 4 February 1928
A group of lads arrived and sent on to Putaruru.

SHIP: SS CORINTHIC

Arrived: Wellington 28 August 1928

36 lads arrived with Adjutant and Mrs George Pratt. Most going on to farms and some to Putaruru.

1 December 1928

An article in the NZ *War Cry* about The Salvation Army chartered ship SS VEDIC which took 500 new settlers to Australia.

22 December 1928

Christmas issue of the NZ *War Cry* with a double page article 'Lads of the Empire' and the training work at Putaruru. An extensive account with several personal examples of trainees' life in the UK and at Putaruru.

SHIP: SS CORINTHIC

Arrived: 19 January 1929

A party of 45 immigrants, 37 of them boys and a woman with 6 children who had been entrusted to The Salvation Army's care by her husband. Major Middlemass is to buy, furnish and set up a house for this family. Lieut-Colonel Frank Barnard (age 66) was the conductor. The boys will be under the care of Captain Ernest Sampson in Putaruru farm.

SHIP: (not recorded)

Arrived: 2 February 1929

A part of 40 lads arrived and went straight to Putaruru.

SHIP: SS ROTORUA

Arrived: 17 August 1929

Commandant S. Cotterill was the conductor of a party of 33 lads.

SHIP: SS RIMUTAKA

Arrived: 17 August 1929

This vessel left England on 5 July 1929 with 33 lads and Staff Captain Herbert Parsons was the conductor. The *War Cry* reports that the immigrants were welcomed at Auckland Congress Hall by Adjutant and Mrs H. Goffin and were present on Sunday night on their way to Putaruru. Alexander J. Grant (age 19) arrived on this vessel but thought he had joined the military and was surprised to find himself at Hadleigh Farm, training to be a farmer. He later went into training as a Salvation Army officer in NZ. (See separate entry)

SHIP: SS TAINUI

Arrived: Wellington 25 January 1930

30 lads arrived with Envoy Alexander Noakes as their conductor. They went on to Putaruru.

SHIP: SS MATAROA

Arrived: 10 May 1930

35 lads arrived with Envoy Arthur Tovey (age 39) as conductor. They are to go to Putaruru for three months training, following which they will be in the Army's care for 3 years, looked after in the event of sickness or unemployment.

29 November 1930

The NZ *War Cry* publishes an extensive article on the training work at Putaruru Farm. Officers and employees are mentioned. Major Charles Fitness, Ensign Chirnsire, Ensign Bicknell, Captain Baker, Lieutenant Ingerson, Sergeant Stevens, Sergeant-Major Mounce, Ensign and Mrs Groves, Lieutenant Boyes, Mrs Ensign Buckingham, Adjutant Edward Bower.

There appears to be no reference to the Immigration scheme and any arrivals during 1931 in the *War Cry*. A comment by Cyril Bradwell states, 'The depression years must have put a stop to the immigration scheme'.

Australia
THE OUTBACK
MAGAZINE

The Salvation Army Migration Department in Australia produced a magazine for the immigrants so they could keep in touch. These are some extracts from the July 1930 edition, Volume 2 issue 7 – the magazine was donated by Major Margaret Lucas.

To the Pioneers from the Old Country
A letter of greeting with the above heading was the first two pages of this issue from Lieut-Commissioner W.J. Barnard Turner, The Army's Director of Migration, London, England. The magazine contained articles and poems as well as keeping in touch comments.

Adjutant Slee of Perth, Western Australia writes about Norman Reeson who came on the ss *Vedic* in 1927. *'In my interview with the above, it will interest you to know that he has banked £100 and sent another £50 home to assist his parents in the Homeland and has a further £19 for his holiday. He is delighted with the country, climate, work and prospects'.*

David Pomfret, ss *Vedic* 1925, called at the Office to inform us that he had been in Ballarat on his honeymoon; he had married a farmer's daughter. He has taken up working on his own farm, which consists of 145 acres, the large part of which is under crop. He also has ten cows.

Horace Matthews, ss *Baradino* 1927, writes to say he is making good progress and looks forward to the magazine each month.

Harry Porter, ss *Vedic* 1927, has just had a well earned holiday in Melbourne and has returned to the country. Mr Ward, his employer, and another man in the district, are giving Harry work between them until things brighten up.

Stanley Hall, ss *Vedic* 1926 is in Melbourne and waiting a position at shearing.

Edward Rogers, ss *Vedic* 1927, writes; *'Always glad to get the Mag and expect others are the same, would like to hear from any chums of the Vedic 1927. I am doing all right and see no reason not to continue to do so. I am wondering how many of you remember what you did on your first day in the first job. Well, I played cricket!*

We regret to hear from Western Australia of the accidental death of William Barr, ex *Berrima* July 1928. William came to this country ahead of his parents who have since settled in Kondinin. Adjutant Slee tried to bring comfort to the sorrowing, which they much appreciated.

Cecil Fenn has changed his position, owing to the depression; he is now at Pymble.

Bert Townsend telephoned to say he is 'Happy as Larry' in his new position at Strathfield.

Thomas Main and his chum Robert Stuart have written to say they are both happy and doing well in their positions on the South Coast.

Harry Wilkinson tells us that his 'Chooks' have the flu.

Cyril Pratt writes to say thank you for the Magazine, and that one of his best pals is in NSW, and he now has his address and is writing to him. Also glad to hear Cecil Fenn and Bert Cox are doing well. He hopes more from the ss *Themistocles* will get in touch.

Canada
IMMIGRATION SCHEME

The Canadian Heritage Centre in Toronto, has the names of nearly forty vessels (recorded) that brought immigrants to Canada until as late as 1932. About 250,000 immigrants arrived in Canada under The Salvation Army Immigration Scheme.

SHIP: SS VICTORIA
Arrived: 5 April 1913
16 Colonists from Hadleigh arrived and were sent to various destinations in Nova Scotia and Ontario. Their ages were from 21 up to 42 years.

SHIP: SS ASCANIA
Arrived: 13 April 1913
17 Colonists from Hadleigh arrived and were mainly heading for postings in Ontario. Their ages ranged from 22 years to 42 years.

SHIP: SS FRANCONIA
Arrived: 4 June 1913
10 Colonists from Hadleigh were aboard this vessel heading for Ontario and Quebec, one is listed as ' did not arrive'

SHIP: SS LAURENTIC
Arrived: 27 July 1913
(no list of names available)

SHIP: SS SCOTIAN
Arrived: 16 June 1913

SHIP: SS LETITIA
This ship left Liverpool on 15 August 1926 and arrived in Quebec (no arrival date recorded). Fifteen year old Leslie Pindred who was on board having been refused by the Australian authorities on the grounds of physical fitness, was accepted into Canada. He became a Salvation Army officer and later was appointed Chief Secretary to the Australian East Territory, in the very country that had turned him down as a lad of 15. (See separate entry)

SHIP: SS ATHENIA
Arrived: 26 June 1932

The Salvation Army Industrial and Land Colony.

LEIGH PARK RECEIVING HOME, HADLEIGH, ESSEX.

PROBATIONER'S DECLARATION AND AGREEMENT.

I, the undersigned, hereby declare that in consequence of my homeless, friendless and destitute condition, or other circumstances set forth in the annexed schedule, I desire to be enrolled as a Probationer for work on the Training Farm of the Industrial and Land Colony; and I declare that the scheduled information is true in substance and in fact, and embodies all material facts affecting my past life, which I am now anxious to reform.

I therefore voluntarily agree to the following terms and conditions of admission, which I fully understand and appreciate, namely :—

1. To submit unconditionally to all the Rules and Regulations which exist now, or may hereafter be framed, *and particularly* to a thorough cleansing of the body and an examination of my clothing. If in the opinion of the Officer-in-charge the latter is considered useless, it may be destroyed or held in reserve at his discretion.

2. Whatever clothing may be deemed necessary for my work and personal comfort shall be supplied to me *on loan*, and can only become *my* property by concession, in writing, from the Governor.

3. Should I leave the Training Farm, taking such clothing with me without first obtaining a written concession, I render myself liable to prosecution for theft.

4. In the event of any breach of this agreement resulting in my having to leave, I fully understand that I shall only be entitled to the clothing which was on my person at the time of my arrival, unless I may have legitimately acquired new clothing of my own ; and should my said clothing have been destroyed, I agree to accept in substitution such garments as the Officer-in-charge thinks fit to provide me with.

5. Under no circumstances, other than set forth in Clause 2, can I claim proprietorship of any boots or wearing apparel that may have been voluntarily supplied to me as necessary to my comfort and work, neither can I prefer any claim for clothing that may have been destroyed in terms of Clause 1.

6. This agreement shall remain in force for a period of three months from the date hereof, and until the expiration of that term I will not apply for outside work, neither will I ask, or expect. other remuneration than *food and shelter* in return for my labour ; the object of this contract being to afford me an opportunity of redeeming my character, regaining strength, and eventually becoming a useful and trustworthy man.

Salvation Army Probationer's Declaration and Agreement. (Reproduced by Courtesy of the Essex Record Office.)

220. Probationer's Declaration. Men were expected to remain on the colony for up to six months, but experience showed that longer stays were necessary. Before accepted, each man had to sign this declaration, voluntarily agreeing to the terms of admission.

7. Throughout the entire term of three months' probation I agree that I will not attempt to leave the precincts of the Training Farm, without written permission, and that no such permission shall be asked for until at least one-half of the term is expired.

8. Under no circumstances will I take intoxicating drink, neither will I at any time enter licensed premises.

9. I will at all times be subservient to the Officer-in-charge, and to those who may be placed in authority over me, whether at work, or in the Dining-room or Dormitory.

10. I shall, however, be at liberty at any time during the said period of three months' probation to apply, through the Officer-in-charge, in writing or otherwise, for a transfer to the Main Colony, which the Governor may give effect to without vitiating, except at his discretion, any of the conditions of this agreement.

11. Should the Governor decline to accede to such application he may, or may not, state his reasons for so doing; in any event the application may be renewed every twenty-one days.

12. At the expiration of the term covered by this agreement it shall be at the absolute discretion of the Governor as to whether I shall be transferred to the Main Colony or required to seek employment elsewhere; and in the event of my being transferred to the Main Colony such transfer shall be based upon an extended agreement for a further period of three months, remuneration to be proportionate to work accomplished, conditional always upon my conduct being satisfactory.

13. I fully understand that, during my residence on the Colony, I must strictly adhere to *all* RULES and REGULATIONS controlling and governing the lives of Colonists; and I bind myself to attend the Saturday evening Roll-call meetings, whether held at Leigh Park or on the Main Colony. I also agree to attend regulation Sunday meetings, and such other religious or social gatherings as may from time to time be arranged, *unless granted exemption by the Officer-in-charge*.

14. For any infringement of Rules, negligence of work, disobedience, or other misconduct, I render myself liable to instant dismissal, and fully understand that such dismissal shall thereafter be a barrier to my re-admission, either to the Training Farm, or Main Colony. This condition also applies in the event of my leaving secretly, or without due regard to the terms and conditions of this agreement.

15. In all matters affecting this agreement or its interpretation the Governor for the time being shall be sole arbiter, and his decision shall be final and binding.

I HEREBY DECLARE that I have read, or have had read to me, the preceding Rules and Conditions, and thoroughly understand them.

Signed..

Date ....

SOME PERSONAL STORIES OF THOSE WHO EMIGRATED TO THE COLONIES AFTER THEIR TIME AT HADLEIGH.

The illustrated guide to the Hadleigh Farm Colony published in 1926 contained some letters describing the experiences of a number of men and boys who had passed through Hadleigh before settling overseas. Since the publication of that guide other stories have come to light and these are a few. The authors would be interested to hear of any others.

This is Andy's story as written by Major Lily Sampson, and published by The Salvation Army in Australia.

Andy came from Yorkshire and was born in 1863, just two years before William Booth began his work with the East London Christian Mission. His father was a tenant farmer and Andy himself, at the age of 16, began work for Mr. Pettigrew, another farmer. Three years after this he discovered that his friend's brother-in-law had been injured in riots against The Salvation Army in Sheffield when William Booth was visiting that city. After a syndicate took over the farm where Andy was working, he was laid off. For a year he was out of work before moving to Liverpool to try to get work in the docks. It was here that Andy had his first experience of getting drunk and also getting lost in the city streets. Eventually he found himself standing opposite a Salvation Army men's shelter where he was able to stay. In the shelter he saw a poster advertising William Booth's Darkest England Scheme. The year was 1889 and on New Year's Eve Staff Captain David Lamb arrived at the hostel to speak about the scheme and appeal for volunteers to take part. All that was needed, he explained, was one pound to guarantee a passage to Canada or Australia. The rest of the fares would be found from funds already subscribed to the scheme. Captain Lamb also pointed out the rules to be observed by anybody wishing to take part. These included no smoking or drinking, no bad language nor any conduct calculated to demoralise the person taking part, and finally no refusal to work. When Captain Lamb returned to the hostel William Booth was about to set up his farm colony at Hadleigh, although at that stage some people were still under the impression that it was Hadleigh, Suffolk that the General had in mind. Captain Lamb wrote on the blackboard what the scheme would involve. This included training in agriculture, spiritual and physical training, welfare and recreation, farming and stock-raising, and work in a market garden, a nursery and glasshouses.

In August 1891 Andy and his friend Todd were told that thay had been chosen to go to Hadleigh. The Sergeant and the Major at the hostel helped them with their train fares so that they could go home first.

Andy's own words describe the next part of the story. 'Down in London it was rush and hurry, but a Captain was waiting for us. He did not know us, nor did we know him but nobody could mistake his red guernsey with "The Salvation Army" in yellow letters across the chest, nor the wide grin when we said "Hadleigh men, sir!"

He took us to a London shelter that night and back came all the memories of our hard times in Liverpool. There were over 30 of us in that dormitory and some tossed, or snored, or groaned, and the watchman came round a couple of times with his lantern, but I warmed up and slept.

There can be no green in all the world better than that sloping land down to the blue water at Hadleigh. We came down in a farm wagon, half a dozen lads from the train, and there it was, smooth in the morning light, and the castle standing on the highest part like it was watching still over the fields.

I was going to stay here! No foggy smoke, no screeching noise, and no more shivering and standing idle in the bitter wind and rain and sleet at a dockyard gate. I was man wanted here. I had got a bit soft on bad living but soon my muscles hardened, and I lifted and chopped and drained and sawed with the best of them. I helped the carpenters build big dormitories for us men and cottages for the staff.'

After a few months at Hadleigh, Andy joined a party of 50 men, some from the City Colonies to sail for Australia on the *Empress of Britain*. They were seen off at the quayside by Colonel Lamb, now the Governor of the Colony, and William Booth. Eventually after a long journey though the Mediterranean and the Suez Canal, the ship arrived at Freemantle in Western Australia. Here the ship was met by two officers who offered work to six men from the London Shelter. However four of those had already jumped ship in search of the gold that had been the main topic of conversation on the journey to Australia. Of the rest of the group seven were bound for Adelaide, 18 for Melbourne, 15 for Sydney and seven for Brisbane, including Andy and his friend Todd. At Brisbane there was a welcome meal in the Brisbane Temple Corps after which Andy set out by train for Ipswich, with the rest of the journey being by wagon and horse. He was put to work with Mr. Southwell but failed to settle there and left the farm with his new friend Charlie, getting work wherever they could, but spending most of their money on drink. This became Andy's life for the next five years. Finally he arrived in the little town of Millthorpe where he got a job in a slaughter yard. Here he built his own cabin but was very lonely. He was often in trouble and on one occasion found himself in a police cell.

He discovered that William Booth was to visit Sydney and decided to take the train in order to hear the General speak. He believed it would make a difference to the way he was living. However when an appeal was made in the public meeting Andy failed to respond, left the building and went back home. A later visit by the Marechale, William Booth's daughter, attracted Andy's attention and he decided to go to hear her preach. It took him two weeks to get to Toowoomba where she was speaking, but although he attended her meeting he once again left before the end.

Back home in Millthorpe, Andy was aware that there was a small Salvation Army Corps but paid it little attention. At the age of 69 he was standing listening to their open-air service, and on this occasion sober enough to hear what they were saying. He followed them back to their hall and made a decision to join them and become a Salvationist. He managed to stay away from the use of alcohol and became part of the Corps fellowship. He proved to be one of the most reliable and useful members of the Millthorpe Corps. A number of years later Captain Lily Samson who had been the Corps Officer in Millthorpe, when Andy decided to become a Salvationist, was appointed to The Salvation Army Training College in Sydney. She discovered that Andy was also now in Sydney, but at the age of eighty-two was living in the Lidcombe State Home for men. The Major, as she now was, visited Andy, but shortly after was told that he had died. In September 1945 Major Sampson conducted his funeral service. He was buried in the Rookwood Methodist Cemetery.

LESLIE PINDRED

Adapted from his own autobiography *A Citizen of Heaven*, and his daughter Paula's account of his life entitled *Happy Adventurer*.

Leslie Pindred was born in Inverness, Scotland in 1911 to Salvation Army officer parents. When his mother died at the early age of forty his father resigned his commission as an officer and Leslie was placed in a Boys' Home. He began to attend the Primitive Methodist church but one day went with his father, with whom he had been reunited, to hear The Salvation Army's Chief of Staff, Commissioner Higgins. This, Leslie said, marked a turning point in his young life and he became increasingly involved with The Salvation Army.

Soon after Leslie became a pupil at Retford Grammar School his father surprised him by asking him if he thought he was brave enough to go to Australia. His father explained that he himself wanted to take advantage of William Booth's 'Darkest England' scheme and emigrate to Australia, but he wanted Leslie to be the forerunner and become the family's pioneer.

His journey began at Doncaster railway station where his father saw him off on the train to London. After crossing the capital he took a train to Leigh-on-Sea, eventually arriving at the Hadleigh Land and Industrial Colony. Leslie's great adventure had begun. He remembered joining a large group of boys 'in a session hundreds strong,' of whom only a few were Salvationists. He met Staff-Captain Swallow but said later that the rest of his memories of Hadleigh were somewhat vague. 'I remember only vaguely the large flock of sheep, the cattle and market garden. We learned to milk cows, hoe vegetables, harvest hay and a score of other things in readiness to be farmers overseas. The food was plain but plentiful. We teased those in charge about its quality and the spending money we received for our work. To the tune of 'The Happy Land' we used to sing;

> 'There is a happy land down Hadleigh way
> Where we get bread and jam three times a day.
> Ham and eggs we never see, we get sawdust in our tea
> And we're gradually fading away down Hadleigh way'

However Leslie's training 'sandwiched into a sort of a crash course about five weeks long' came to a bitterly disappointing conclusion. He had dreamed of nothing else but becoming an Australian. Then he was told at fourteen and a half years that he had not reached the physical requirements demanded by the Australian government. His options were either to go home for a year, presumably to put on weight, or to accept a passage to Canada. Finally on 15 August 1926 he sailed from England on board the liner *Letitia* and arrived in Quebec. After spending some time in Smith Falls Ontario he was sent to a farm near Stittsville in the Ottawa Valley. He worked for the Dawson family who belonged to the Plymouth Brethren, and after High School, went to The Salvation Army Training College for Officers in Toronto in 1932.

When Leslie's daughter Paula took up his story she spoke about her father's parents-in-law, Harry and Daisy Everett, who both came from Essex. Daisy came from Southend and Harry from the nearby village of Great Wakering. In 1913 Daisy and Harry left Essex to begin a new life in Toronto. In 1918 they entered the Toronto Training College for Officers and were sent in charge of the corps at Smith Falls. It was from this corps many years later that their daughter Alma and Leslie also entered the Toronto Training College. Leslie and Alma were married and after various Canadian appointments Leslie was sent to the Australia Eastern Territory to become its Chief Secretary. Forty-two years after his first abortive attempt to reach Australia he had finally arrived. The year was 1968.

Leslie Pindred's final Salvation Army appointments were as a territorial commander, first in Holland and finally back in Australia. The irony perhaps would not be lost on Commissioner Pindred that the country which had refused him entry as an underweight 14 year old now welcomed him as the highest ranking Salvation Army officer for the Australia Eastern territory.

Commissioner Leslie Pindred died in 2000.

THE STORY OF
ALEXANDER JOHN WILLIAM GRANT – 'SCOTTY'

Alexander Grant was born in July 1910, just two years before the death of William Booth. He came from a very poor family in Carrbridge in the north of Scotland. His father died when he was six, and his stepfather was an alcoholic. As a teenager Alexander seemed destined to follow in his stepfather's footsteps. However when he was 17 he saw an advertisement for a young men's emigration scheme to Australia and New Zealand. He applied, thinking The Salvation Army was some form of military organisation. When he discovered it was a religious group he thought they were 'the daftest group of people I had ever seen,' Despite this he travelled to Hadleigh to take part in the training course, having received the details from The Salvation Army in Aberdeen. On his way to Hadleigh he passed through London where he was told to look out for a man in a blue uniform. The man in a blue uniform turned out to be a policeman who told him to "wait here and sooner or later you will see a Salvationist" and so I did.'

At Hadleigh in 1929 he joined 130 other boys all with the same idea of making their fortunes overseas. He stayed at Hadleigh for six weeks, which was 'a totally new experience to me, a raw country lad from a poor home, kept poor too by a father's addiction to alcohol and a large family.' Alexander sailed from England on the ss *Rimataka* bound for The Salvation Army Training Farm at Putaruru. He described his arrival at the farm on a very wet weekend. 'It seemed like the end of the world. We were surrounded by bush and mud and had to walk the last three miles. We were put to various work and my first job in New Zealand was planting potatoes. I liked horses and stock and possibly as a consequence I was asked to stay on as an employee at the end of my training, at the privileged wage of two New Zealand dollars a week. For four years I worked there and I may say my recollections of those years are lots of hard work, wonderful friends, and above all the fact that on 12 July 1931, after a period of real heart searching and conviction, I gave myself over to the Lord Jesus Christ in the little hall at the Hodderville Boys' Home. The choice I made that night was the best I ever made. Some two to three years after I felt I should be an officer despite a strong desire to make my fortune and return home.' He left Cambridge (NZ) Corps in March 1935 to enter The Salvation Army Training College in Wellington where he remained for two years. He stayed there for a further year before being appointed to Matamata corps. After his marriage to Captain Linda Proctor he had two more corps appointments before moving to Putaruru Training Farm in 1940, 11 years after he had arrived there to taste farming life in New Zealand for the first time. Many more appointments were to follow; experiencing both corps and the Army's varied Social Work in New

Zealand. Brigadier Grant retired in 1975. He died in July 2000 at the age of 90. Little did he know, when he set out from Scotland to Hadleigh all those years before, to link up with what he believed to be a strange military organisation, where his remarkable journey would lead. 'Scotty' Grant's story is one that has been recorded. How many others still wait to be told?

Carry this in your pocket on the journey

How to get to

HADLEIGH

(ESSEX)

TRAINING

FARMS ::

HOW TO GET TO HADLEIGH (Essex) TRAINING FARMS

It is important to leave home in time to arrive in London by 3 o'clock in the afternoon. This will give you sufficient time to cross London. Immediately on arrival make for Fenchurch Street Station, so that you may depart by the train leaving at seven minutes past four. For 'How to cross London' see instructions on the next page.

An Army Officer will be present at Fenchurch Street Station. Make yourself known to him. He is there to guide you and will see that you travel by the right train. He will supply you (at our cost) with a special privilege ticket.

After a run of about one hour look out for the ruins of Hadleigh Castle (on the left), Southend Pier (away ahead on the right), and three minutes later you will be at Leigh-on-Sea Station, where you alight. This is the nearest station to the Hadleigh Farm Training Schools. Immediately on coming out of Leigh-on-Sea Station, climb to the top of the hill and there, by the church, you will find a conveyance ready to take you and other lads to Hadleigh.

If your train should be late, or if for any reason you miss connexions and you do not see our Officer, make your own way to Hadleigh. There is a good service of trains from Fenchurch Street to Leigh-on-Sea, from which town there is a regular bus service to Hadleigh.

HOW TO CROSS LONDON

On arrival in London the point to make for first is Mark Lane Station on the Underground Railway.

From Mark Lane Station to Fenchurch Street Station is five minutes' walk. Turn to the right immediately on leaving the station and take the first street on the right. The fine building on the right is the offices of the Port of London Authority (the view you get is of the back of the building). At the end of that short street bear to the left (by an old church) then turn to right. Climb the few steps in front of you and you are at Fenchurch Street Station.

Undernoted are the various big arrival stations in London. You will know which one you arrive at, therefore follow the instructions given against that particular station.

KING'S CROSS. ST. PANCRAS. These are two big stations almost next door to each other. At each there are subways leading some distance underground to King's Cross Underground Station. At the end of the subway book to Mark Lane Station. The fare is a few pence. Then go down the steps to the platform for Eastbound Trains and travel by train labelled 'Inner Circle.' Mark Lane Station is the sixth station, and you will get there in about a quarter of an hour.

EUSTON. MARYLEBONE. On the arrival platforms are subways to Underground tubes. The booking offices are down steps. Book to Mark Lane Station. The fare will be a few pence. Travel by train to Charing Cross. At Charing Cross proceed up the moving staircase which will bring you to Charing Cross Underground Station. Here you go to the platform for Eastbound trains, and any train not labelled 'Mansion House Only' will take you to Mark Lane Station, which is six stations away.

WATERLOO. Proceed by Underground subway, entrance to which is on the station, to Bakerloo Tube booking office. Book to Mark Lane Station, the fare being a few pence. Go down by lift to the platform for Charing Cross. Change at Charing Cross, which is the first station after leaving Waterloo. Go up the moving staircase, which will bring you to Charing Cross Underground Station. Here you go to the platform for Eastbound trains, and any train which is not marked 'Mansion House Only' will take you to Mark Lane Station, six stations away. The whole journey takes about twenty minutes.

CHARING CROSS. Walk down to Charing Cross Underground Station, walk to on the Embankment by the river, which you have crossed before arriving. Book to Mark Lane Station, which will cost a few pence. Go down the steps to the platform for Eastbound trains, and travel by any train not marked 'Mansion House Only.' Mark Lane Station is six stations away, and will be reached in about twelve minutes.

ST. PAUL'S. Underneath St. Paul's Station is Blackfriars Underground Station. Book to Mark Lane Station, which will cost twopence. Travel by any Eastbound train not marked 'Mansion House Only' to Mark Lane Station, four stations away. The journey will take eight or ten minutes.

CANNON STREET. Almost underneath Cannon Street Station is the Underground Railway Cannon Street Station. Book to Mark Lane Station, which is two stations away and will be reached in five minutes. Travel by any Eastbound train, from the Eastbound platform.

---

221. Instruction sheet for getting to Hadleigh Farm Colony. Mark Lane underground station is now known as Tower Hill.

W. BRAMWELL BOOTH, GENERAL.

THE SALVATION ARMY.

IMMIGRATION & SETTLEMENT DEPARTMENT.

OFFICE OF THE RESIDENT SECRETARY:
National Bank Chambers,
Cuba Street,
Wellington, N.Z.

WILLIAM BOOTH, FOUNDER.

TELEPHONE 22·494.

P.O. BOX 136,
TE ARO.

IN YOUR REPLY QUOTE
REFERENCE NUMBER:

THE RESIDENT SECRETARY:
MAJOR A. GREENE.

192

My dear Friend,

      We give you a very hearty welcome to New Zealand, and wish to assure you of our interest in your welfare. You can always rely on us doing our best for you.

      We would like to draw your attention to the conditions of service under which you came out to this Country.

      As to wages, lads who are placed direct from the boat receive 15/- a week and lodging and blankets, with a rise to £1 after about three months. Lads trained at Putaruru are placed at £1 a week. These figures however, are not binding; if you are not alert, willing, and teachable, the employer may give you less, and you would have no choice but to accept it. Of this you will receive 5/- weekly for pocket money, and we advise you to put it to good use. The employer will send the balance to this Office to pay off your loan. After this has been met we will bank it for you at 4% interest, until such times as we release you, and this will be determined by the way you prove yourself as a money-saver.

      If you are in need of clothes, arrange with your employer and he will buy them for you, deducting the cost from the monthly cheque, sending us the receipts in lieu of cash. When changing places for any reason, always inquire of your employer if he has sent in your wages up to date, and, if not, inform us at once.

      No lad must leave a place without our permission. A week's notice must be given on either side. If a lad leaves without a week's notice he forfeits a week's wages, if the employer puts a lad off without a week's notice he must pay a week's wages in lieu thereof.

      The length of term depends upon the suitability of the place, but it is very desirable that lads stay for at least twelve months. If a lad can show that it is not suitable and that the request to shift is reasonable, then we will find another place. Never fail to notify us, immediately after arrival at a new place.

      Here are a few general rules that we would like you to remember: — be good at getting up early in the morning, watch how the employer moves round and pick up his stride, listen to what is told you, be keen to learn, be courteous, cheerful, not easily offended, straight-forward, truthful, clean in your language, and in your appearance, and be a gentleman at all times. Put your trust in God, and make up your mind that you will succeed and make good in this Country.

      May God bless you and guide you.

           Yours faithfully,

                          MAJOR,
                          RESIDENT SECRETARY.

222. A letter of welcome to New Zealand which also sets out the conditions and rules governing the emigration scheme.

A. & N.Z.   Putaruru for training. (Training 30/5/29). **CONFIDENTIAL**

The Salvation Army Boys' Scheme
(UNDER EMPIRE SETTLEMENT ACT, 1922)

STATEMENT

furnished by The Salvation Army for the information of boys going to Australia and New Zealand under the above scheme, showing the costs of training, outfitting, and transportation, and how the costs are met. This statement is given to the boy when his training is completed and after he has been finally approved for sailing.

TO   G.9325. GRANT. Allister.   (Name of Boy)

The cost of assisting you to proceed to $\frac{\text{Australia}}{\text{New Zealand}}$ is as follows :

		£	s.	d.
1.	Railway fares in the United Kingdom		11	2
2.	Maintenance and instruction at the Hadleigh Farm (calculated at 30s. per week)	7	18	7
3.	Outfit provided	18		
4.	Ocean Passage—Boys under 17	6		
	Boys over 17	33		
5.	Rail fare in $\frac{\text{Australia}}{\text{New Zealand}}$ (free rail)	1		
6.	Incidental expenses of the journey (including food on train overseas, insurance of baggage, &c.)		10	
	TOTAL £	67	5	9

(Item 2: Weeks 5 Days 2; 12 — in N.Z.)

HOW THE ABOVE EXPENSES ARE MET

			£	s.	d.			
You have contributed						5	12	6
The British Government has promised to contribute towards item 1	£	s. 3	d. 8					
,, ,, 2	10	4	3					
,, ,, 3	3							
,, ,, 4 & 5	16	10						
,, ,, 6		7	6					
Total	30	5	5	30	5	5		
The $\frac{\text{Australian}}{\text{New Zealand}}$ Government has promised to contribute towards item 2								
,, ,, 4 & 5	16	10						
Total	16	10		16	10			

*The Australian Government has loaned you ..

*The Salvation Army has loaned you ..
(* This loan will be recovered from your wages after arrival overseas, in accordance with the undertaking signed by you.)

	£	s.	d.
Total	52	7	11

The balance of the cost has to be found by The Salvation Army, which has also incurred expenses not included in the above statement in connexion with your selection and which may have arisen from your medical examination in this country. Further expenses in connexion with supervision and after-care will also have to be incurred, for these The Army are responsible as well as for training (if any) after arrival overseas in Australia and New Zealand.

Towards the above expenses you have agreed to contribute a further amount of £5 10s. 0d. in the case of those proceeding to Australia and New Zealand out of your wages when at work overseas. This is in addition to any loan made by The Salvation Army or by the Government in the case of boys proceeding to Australia.

General Booth feels that the boys assisted by The Army will be glad to contribute in this way so that The Salvation Army may be able to continue its work in training and assisting other boys to settle overseas.

1,000—5.28—C.P.—3891—o/OA/E

223. A breakdown of the costs of the emigration scheme and how they are met.

Alexander's diary.

Alexander kept a daily diary from the time he left home in Scotland until his arrival in New Zealand. After that the diary records many of his experiences in his new country. The following are some extracts from this diary.

24 May 1929. Last day of work in Scotland.

30 May. Arrived at Hadleigh at 11.40 a.m. *after an overnight journey from Scotland to London.* After dinner had a lecture about the rules of the Colony.

31 May. Got up at 5.30 a.m. Breakfast at 6. Line up in front of mess room. March off to work. Supper at 5p.m. followed by a game of football and in bed by 8.30.

Saturday 1 June. Finished work at 12.30p.m. After a dinner of beef and potatoes, pudding and a cup of coffee walked to Leigh. In the evening had lecture in Citadel.

Other entries highlight the work involved. This included digging potatoes, cutting thistles in the cornfield, sawing logs, feeding and cleaning the pigs, marking sheep with red paint and cutting their toenails.

Tuesday 6 June. Weight and height taken. Passed by the doctor.

Tuesday 11 June. Working in men's dining room. Scrubbing floors, washing dishes and peeling potatoes.

Monday 17 June. Working in the laundry. Washing socks, turning the washing machine and stoking the fires. Later in the day walked up to Hadleigh village to get rubber soles on my shoes.

Tuesday 18 June. All the New Zealand boys got their photographs taken and had a letter from the doctor.

Friday 21 June. Vaccinated today,

Friday 28 June. Twenty three boys left for Canada.

Thursday 4 July. All New Zealand boys have to go and get their tickets and pack their cases.

Friday 5 July. Up at 5a.m. After breakfast by bus for Leigh. Train to London and another train to Southampton. Boarded the ship at 11.45a.m. The boat left at 2.30p.m. Very seasick.

Monday 8 July. *Today's entry shows a typical day on board.* Up at 7a.m. Breakfast at 8. Got tennis shoes and cricket shirt to wear on board. Played games e.g. draughts. Dinner at 12.30p.m. Roast beef and pudding. In the afternoon played games and chased one another. Tea at 5p.m. followed by a sing-song. Supper at eight, cheese and biscuits. Bed 9.30.

Wednesday 10 July. Did two hours work today cleaning brass in the ship's snooker room.

Friday 12 July. Had our photographs taken and got one shilling from a Salvation Army officer and some sweets.

Monday 22 July; keeping a sharp lookout for land. First seen at 2.30p.m.

8.15p.m. landed in a motor launch, had a look round the town, bought a bunch of bananas. Left the shore at 12.45a.m. and in bed by 1-o-clock.

Tuesday 23 July. Up at first light to see the boat entering the Panama Canal. Passed through three locks. The passage through the canal lasted from 6a.m. to 3p.m. Saw the last of America about 7p.m. A wonderful journey, if only it had been cooler. Saw a lot of native huts and villages beside fruit trees of every kind. *(Alexander continues to speak about an enjoyable cruise*

Tuesday 13 August. Short lecture on New Zealand in the evening.

Thursday 15 August. Expect to land at Auckland tomorrow. Crossed the one hundred and eighty degrees meridian, therefore tomorrow will not exist. We are now halfway around the world and have lost a day.

Saturday 17 August; saw land about 7.30a.m. Got into harbour at 3p.m. Had a walk round the town after tea.

Monday 19 August. Had breakfast in one of the tea-rooms in the town, belonging to one of The Salvation Army officers. Jolly fine breakfast. Left by train at 10a.m. and arrived at Putaruru station at 3.15 p.m. Taken to the farm and had tea.

Tuesday 20 August. Two of us had to peel potatoes. My first job in New Zealand.

The rest of Alexander's diary describes his work and life in his new country. His work included digging in the garden, planting onions, making butter, digging drains and road making.

Tuesday 27 August. Got 2/6d from the Captain.

Wednesday 28 August. Sixteen degrees of frost this morning.

Friday 30 August. All the boys changed jobs today. I am in the dairy and driving a cart with two horses.

Saturday 31 August. Got up at 4a.m. Milking till 6a.m. Milking again from 3p.m.till 6p.m.

Alexander's diary continues to record various jobs he did. His final entries include;

Tuesday 8 October. Two letters from home, one posted 25 August and one 1 September.

Friday 11 October. Changed jobs today. I am now on the four-horse team.

Saturday 12 October. Ploughing with a double furrow with four horses.

Thursday 17 October. Down at Putaruru at a Maori concert tonight. Very good and well worth hearing.

This day to day account of a young emigrant's journey to and the first few weeks in New Zealand, gives a fascinating glimpse of how one young man saw this opportunity for a new life in a new land.

THE STORY OF EDDIE CAKEBREAD

Written by his son Keith

Eddie was born into a working class family during the reign of Edward V11. Having left school in 1921 he went to work for Carter Paterson as a messenger boy in the City of London. However by the age of 16 Eddie was looking for something more out of life than running messages for other people. He came across an advertisement asking for 'Boys for the Empire.' This was a scheme offering to help young men emigrate to Britain's overseas colonies to be trained in farming. Eddie had two uncles who had already emigrated; they were known as 'the rich uncles in Australia.' He discovered that the scheme was organised by The Salvation Army. He might well have seen their advertisement in their Migration Office in Upper Thames Street, close to where he worked.

He didn't come from a religious background, but the Army stressed that the applicant's religious beliefs or lack of them was not a problem. The important criteria were the boy's age, between 14 and 18 (later extended to 19), a medical certificate from his doctor, two referees and parental consent. It was this last item that was Eddie's problem; his father was totally opposed to the idea. Eddie would have to wait until he came of age at 21 and was able to make up his own mind. However he didn't have to wait that long, thanks to the intervention of his aunt Polly, his father's favourite sister. His father relented, and the application forms were duly dispatched. To Eddie's delight the reply came that he had been accepted for farm training in Australia. He was told to bring 'good, old clothes and one or two pairs of strong boots'. Since that was all he had anyway, it was no problem. The Army's strict rules about drinking, smoking and general discipline didn't worry him too much.

He was told to report to the Hadleigh Farm Colony within a week. It gradually began to dawn on him that his decision to emigrate, however exciting it was, was likely to be a question of burning his boats, and that he might never see his family again. He was to meet the rest of his training group at Bow Road in the east end of London and travel down to Hadleigh with them.

In later life he spoke little about his time at Hadleigh. It seems likely he didn't enjoy it very much. Almost 19, and at the upper end of the age group he probably found the religious-based discipline irksome. One of his concerns was that although he was taught many trades he was not taught to ride. Towards the end of his training, doctors and immigration officials from the different dominions came down to Hadleigh to inspect the potential emigrants. Unfortunately for Eddie he failed the Australian test as being small and too skinny. However New

Zealand was willing to accept him. He was almost certainly not the first nor the last to fail the rather stricter Australian requirements.

Early in September 1926 Eddie joined a group of boys under the leadership of Major Bennett who set out from Leigh-on-Sea station on the first stage of their long journey to the other side of the world. At Southampton they joined nearly seven hundred other passengers to board a New Zealand ship the ss *Tamaroa*. Just before the ship docked at Wellington Major Bennett arranged for each of the boys to be presented with a Salvation Army Bible, a personal gift from General Bramwell Booth. This event did not seem to have impressed the young immigrant, more interested probably in taking his first steps on New Zealand soil. After leaving the ship Eddie had to pass through immigration control where he had to answer many questions. The most unexpected came from a New Zealand military sergeant, who gave Eddie a document setting out his military obligations. This meant that all young male immigrants would become Territorial Reservists in the New Zealand Army with a number of hours of military training to be completed each year. Eddie was sure this was the first time he had heard about this requirement. Had The Salvation Army omitted or forgotten to tell him?

His next step was to be introduced to a couple who were to be his local patrons. This patronage was arranged by The Salvation Army. They were normally a married couple who had volunteered to make sure that the young immigrant settled into his new life as quickly as possible. They would be a kind of surrogate mother and father. Eddie was asked to write to them periodically to let them know how he was getting on. They lived in Wellington. He had been found employment by The Salvation Army as a trainee farmhand near Morrinsville near Auckland. The Salvation Army had also arranged his travel for the 400 mile journey northwards.

Eddie's new employer was George Marshall whom he got on with straight away. He would be paid ten shillings a week in addition to his board and meals. Out of this weekly wage he was expected to repay The Salvation Army up to £19 pounds; the cost of his training and travel. Eddie seemed to take an instant liking to his life in New Zealand. He liked the people, the countryside, the vastness and the newness of everything. He learnt how to milk cows by hand which became his permanent job. He also learnt how to ride. During the next few years he worked on a number of farms and in the autumn of 1931 he was given work by a farmer called Gordon Forlong. When Eddie arrived at this new farm he had no idea how his life was going to change over the next few months.

Gordon Forlong was a deeply religious man and since Eddie was treated as one of the family he was expected to be present when grace was said at meals and at the Bible reading which followed breakfast time. Eddie became increasingly annoyed with this religious atmosphere but gradually the way that Gordon and his family lived their lives made an increasing impression on him. One day Eddie had what Christians call a Damascus Road experience and from then on became a Christian.

Eddie began to attend the Brethren Hall with the Forlong family but in April

1933 he was back in England. Back home he started to attend the Bethany Hall in Islington, close to where he was now living. In 1945 Eddie Cakebread, together with his wife, moved from London and bought a house in Thundersley, Essex, just a short walking distance form the Hadleigh Farm Colony where he had arrived as a 19 year old trainee farmer nearly twenty years before.

Bibliography

In Darkest England and the Way Out, William Booth, *The Salvation Army. 1890.*

The History of The Salvation Army, Volume Three, Robert Sandall *Nelson and Sons 1955.*

William Booth: Founder of The Salvation Army, Volume two, Harold Begbie, *Macmillan, 1920.*

Booth's Boots: The Beginning of Salvation Army Social Work, Lieut-Colonel Jenty Fairbank, *The Salvation Army, 1983.*

The Story of a Great Endeavour: The Hadleigh Land and Industrial Colony, 1902.

The Illustrated Guide to the Colony, *c.* 1926.

Hadleigh Past, Ian Yearsley, *Phillimore, 1998.*

Hadleigh, M. Hancock and S. Harvey, *Phillimore, 1986.*

Leigh-on-Sea, Judith Williams, *Phillimore, 2002.*

Articles in the Essex Journal, *Mark Sorrell, 1992.*

The Railway at Hadleigh Castle, H.W. Paar, *Journal of the Industrial Railways Society. 1973.*

The Salvation Army Railway, H.W.Paar, *Industrial Railways Record June 1982.*

Articles in the Southend Standard.

A Study of SALIC Farm, Greta Groves, 1956.

Articles in the Australian War Cry. 1927.

Articles in The Salvation Army folder in the Gardens of Easton Lodge Museum.

The Finance Minutes of the Farm Colony,1939 – 1957.

Soldiers of the Cross: Pioneers of Social Change, Susie Swift and David Lamb, Norman Murdoch, *Crest books, The Salvation Army, Virginia, U.S.A. 2006.*

Origins of The Salvation Army, Norman Murdoch, 1994.

Andy – Stranger than Fiction, Lily K. Sampson, *The Salvation Army, Australia, 1999.*

Article in Caps and Bonnets, (*Leigh-on-Sea Corps Magazine*), Roly Little.

Essex: Gateway to Utopia, Dennis Hardy, *Essex Countryside, January 1975.*

Rider Haggard's Report on the Farm Colony, 1905.

Article in the Hadleigh Free Press, Mrs Marjorie Wiedman, February 1985.

The Hadleigh Farm Colony Band Reunion Programme, 1936.

Articles in *The Musician.*

Florence Gardens, Hadleigh, Conservation Area Review and Management Plan, *Essex County Council.*

Hadleigh Colony Citadel/Hadleigh Temple Corps History Book 1937 onwards.

The Historical Bio-Social Influence of The Salvation Army on part of South-East Essex, *Shirley Coulson-Broom 1984.*

The Essex Hundred, Summersbook (UK) Ltd Southend-on-Sea 2006.

Photograph Credits

Derek Barber collection 1, 8, 13, 19, 34, 35, 36, 37, 28, 39, 40, 41, 42, 50, 52, 53, 56, 57, 58, 59, 64, 65, 66, 68, 69, 70, 71, 73, 80, 81, 82, 90, 91, 92, 97, 98, 99, 100, 102, 110 (top), 110, 112, 121, 122, 133, 135, 137, 138, 139, 145. Salvation Army International Heritage Centre 2, 3, 4, 5, 6, 14, 15, 16, 17, 20, 21, 24, 25, 28, 29, 31, 32, 33, 47, 48, 51, 54, 67, 72, 74, 75, 76, 77, 78, 79, 83, 84, 85, 86, 87, 88, 89, 93, 94, 95, 96, 101, 103, 106, 113, 119, 120, 123, 124, 125, 126, 144, 178, 179, 217, 219, front endpaper. Salvation Army Heritage Centre New Zealand 117, 118. Salvation Army Heritage Centre Melbourne 55, 127, 128, 129, 130, 131, 132. Graham Cook 9, 10, 11, 12, 18, 23, 26, 27, 49, 60, 62, 105, 107, 109, 114, 146, 147, 148, 150, 153, 170, 173, 175, 177, 189, 210, 212, 213, 214, 215, back endpaper illustrations. Trustees of Easton Lodge 22. Industrial Railways Record 30. Robin Bryant 160, 180, 181, 182, 183, 184, 185, 186, 187, 188, 190, 191, 192, 193, 196, 198, 199, 201, 202, 203, 204, 205, 206, 209, 207. David Greenwood 43, 45. Alf Lowrey 110 (lower), 136, 168. Deryck Turton 151, 152, 154, 155, 156, 157, 158, 159. Peter Wexham 44, 46. Greta Groves 61, 63. Joyce Swansbury 169. Don Watson 104, 115, 161, 162, 163, 164, 165, 166, 172, 174, 211. Peter Howard 171, 176. Bryan Snow 108, 116, 134, 140, 141, 142, 143. Ayshford Samsome Architects 218. Hadleigh Training Centre 194, 195, 197, 200, 208, 216.

WHAT TO SEE AND DO AT HADLEIGH FARM

The Rare Breeds' Centre is normally open to the public between Easter and October. Individuals, as well as those taking part in educational visits are most welcome.

The Farmers' Markets take place on the second Wednesday of each month apart from January.

The Tea Room is open to the public between 9.30a.m. and 4.00p.m. from Monday to Friday and between 10.00a.m. and 4.00p.m. on Saturday and Sunday.

The Farm and Tea Room are situated in Castle Lane which is the road leading from Hadleigh Town Centre to Hadleigh Castle.

There is car parking at the Farm and disabled access to the Tea Room and Rare Breeds' Centre.

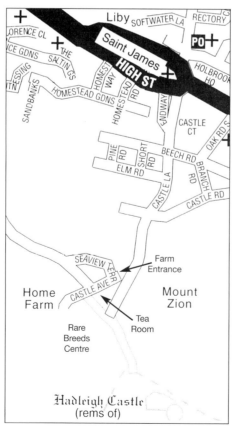

The nearest public transport is along the A 13. There is a bus service to Hadleigh church from both Benfleet and Leigh-on-Sea railway stations.

From the church it is approximately half a mile to the farm entrance.

The telephone number of the Farm is 01702 558550 and the Training Centre is 01702 552963. It is advisable to check opening times of both before travelling.

Farm website:
www.hadleighfarm.co.uk